THE CHICAGO WHITE SOX

WRITING SPORTS SERIES
Richard "Pete" Peterson, Editor

The Cleveland Indians
Franklin Lewis

The Cincinnati Reds
Lee Allen

The Chicago White Sox
Warren Brown

Dreaming Baseball
James T. Farrell

THE CHICAGO

WHITE SOX

WARREN BROWN

THE KENT STATE UNIVERSITY PRESS
KENT, OHIO

Library of Congress Catalog Card Number 2007004891

ISBN-13: 978-0-87338-895-5

Manufactured in the United States of America

11 10 09 08 07   5 4 3 2 1

Library of Congress Cataloging-in-Publication Data

Brown, Warren, b. 1894.

The Chicago White Sox / Warren Brown.

p. cm. — (Writing sports series)

Originally published: New York : Putnam, 1952.

Includes index.

ISBN-13: 978-0-87338-895-5 (pbk. : alk. paper) ∞

1. Chicago White Sox (Baseball team)—History.

2. Baseball—History. I. Title.

GV875.C58B7 2007

796.357'6409773'11—dc22

2007004891

British Library Cataloging-in-Publication data are available.

CONTENTS

Nelson "Nellie" Fox with manager Paul Richards.

FOREWORD

Fifty-two years, the defining tragedy of the Black Sox, and the very best and worst of Chicago's storied South Side baseball team would pass before the complete history of the White Sox could finally be told in book form.

Hard times and losing baseball spanning three decades—book-ended by the Black Sox Scandal of 1920 and the lightning resurgence of a dormant ball club given up for dead in 1950 before the "Miracle of '51"—were the obstacles that stood in the way of the New York publishing world entertaining notions of bringing out the first complete team history.

During that long enduring and bitter thirty-year cycle, when Charles Comiskey's once-proud Chicago White Sox disintegrated from elite status as the pre-Yankee, pre-Ruthian cornerstone franchise of the American League into a perennial doormat that became the butt of standing jokes (John Carmichael, the witty and urbane *Daily News* scribe once suggested that a zoning ordinance be enacted to rename a section of 35th Street adjoining the ballpark to "Seventh Place"), despairing and long-suffering fans accepted the fact that their beloved team had been relegated to second-class standing in America's second city behind the popular and successful Cubs, who had progressed to the World Series in three-year cycles between 1929 and 1938.

When G. P. Putnam's publishing company in New York commissioned some of the nation's most distinguished baseball writers to pen a series of team histories (beginning with the New York Yankees in 1943), the upturn in White Sox fortunes was still years away. The memories of the glorious "Hitless Wonder" years of the early 1900s and the prescandal exploits of that fabled Black Sox team kindled fond remembrances among a graying generation of Chicago baseball enthusiasts who were still around to tell the story of those wonderful days to their grandchildren.

But years of losing and a series of unexpected setbacks on and off the field had taken their toll. The fan base had eroded in the 1920s and 1930s, and many were convinced that a "Comiskey Curse" was afoot—not unlike the fate that had befallen the Boston Red Sox after selling Babe Ruth to the Yankees in 1920. As the team floundered in the lower strata of the American League ahead of, or behind, the Washington Senators, the St. Louis Browns, and the Philadelphia Athletics in any given year, the primary objective of the Comiskey heirs was bare-bones survival.

Drawing 500,000 fans a year to cover the cost of player salaries and operating expenses until a miraculous turnaround or divine intervention, whichever came first, became the singular obsession. In the leanest years of the Great Depression, the club fell well short of even that modest attainment. In 1932, only 233,198 fans passed through the turnstiles.

This was the unhappy state of affairs in the House of Comiskey when Frank Graham and Fred Lieb, two writers whose eyewitness experiences in baseball transcended the Dead Ball era of 1900 up through the budding stardom of Joe DiMaggio and Ted Williams, launched the Putnam series. Graham penned books for the New York teams (Yankees, Dodgers, and Giants) with alacrity. The prolific Lieb, who covered 8,000 major league games during his long and colorful career, wrote seven of the Putnam histories—the Phillies, Red Sox, Pirates, Orioles, Cardinals, As, and Tigers.

However workmanlike and thorough the content of these books were, the missing ingredient in each of them was the important *local* perspective, the intimate and affectionate regard of the author for one team based on years of experience covering that one ball club, kibitzing with the players on and off the beat in the Pullman cars and out-of-town hotels from the start of spring training up through the World Series.

Warren Brown, author of *The Chicago White Sox*, was not a native son of the Windy City, but down to the bone he was every inch a Chicagoan, and more importantly he was a Sox enthusiast. Born in a tough working-class section of San Francisco, Brown's passion for the American Pastime was honed at an early age while swatting around the horsehide with a neighborhood street team known as the Telegraph Hill Boys. Among the recognized alums personally known to Brown in those formative years were Charles "Swede" Risberg and Claude "Lefty" Williams, two of the great players who sold out Comiskey in the darkest days of the Black Sox Scandal.

"I like baseball and baseball writing more than any other," he wrote in his 1947 memoir of the sporting world, titled *Win, Lose or Draw.* "I take what unfolds before my eyes. I am willing to enjoy what I have in sports, and let the dear past as well as the future take care of itself."

Brown, a Latin scholar, famous teetotaler, and convivial after-dinner toastmaster with an encyclopedic knowledge of sports of all sorts, broke into print with the *San Francisco Bulletin* in 1919. He sold his first article, "Baseball Echoes from the Pacific Coast League," to *Baseball Magazine*, a national publication in July of that same year. And so began a prolific writing career that stretched into the late 1960s. In forty years he never missed a Kentucky Derby, and he knew the fight game inside and out. Brown confounded oddsmakers by picking Gene Tunney over Jack Dempsey in the famous 1927 "Long Count" championship bout in Chicago's Soldier Field.

Warren Brown reported for duty at William Randolph Hearst's *Chicago Herald and Examiner* in 1923, after abandoning notions of a professional baseball career in his beloved Pacific Coast League and short reporting stints with the *San Francisco Call-Post* and the *New York Evening Mail,* where he traded barbs and hoisted his stein of ginger ale with the likes of Damon Runyon and the other literary wags of the Great White Way. Fight promoter Jack "Doc" Kearns, the promotional genius behind the great Dempsey, squired Brown around to his customary Manhattan watering holes, introducing his young protégé to the local literati.

One night Runyon elbowed his way past the thirsty throng to meet and greet his old comrade Kearns, then said, "So you're the new fellow from the West Coast?" motioning toward Brown.

"Yes," the young reporter replied. "And what did you say your name was?"

Brown was a loyal and devoted Hearst man for thirty-two of his forty-eight years in the business. In turn, the "Chief" rewarded him with his own column, a breezy collection of anecdotes and observations titled "So They Tell Me," and he easily adapted to the rhythms of life in wide-open, Prohibition-era Chicago.

Through his warm and engaging personality, Brown managed to ingratiate himself with the late-night revelers and show people and would become their confidante in the clubs and downtown hotels they frequented. The lean, angular writer held court each night at the College Inn of the old Hotel Sherman, a landmark hostelry on Randolph

Street that was razed in the 1970s. Joining him for after-hours merriment were the legendary Chicago newspaper-men of the day, whose careers covering the sports beat spanned the 1920s up through the 1970s: Jim Enright, John P. Carmichael, Arch Ward, Irving Vaughn, Dick Hacken-berg, Dan Desmond, Ed Burns, and Gene Kessler.

To their inner circle, Brown and his cohorts welcomed such show business illuminati as Joe E. Lewis, Olsen and Johnson, and other vaudevillians whose job was to amuse and delight in a series of talent shows orchestrated by Brown. Warren Brown loved the roistering good times and all the hob-knobbing no doubt, but he was also a devoted family man who raised three children on the city's South Side.

Writing was his craft, and he was an extraordinarily disciplined and versatile reporter who acknowledged that there was more to it than keeping up with the gossip of ballplay-ers and transcribing box scores. "I've written about every damned thing under the sun," he remarked. "I even did the-atrical and vaudeville reviews." And although he wore many hats in an event-filled career—in the early days of live tele-vision he was a panelist on *Ask Me Another*, a locally produced quiz show where he put his formidable knowledge of sports to the test each week—baseball was always his meal ticket.

In 1946, to capitalize on the Cubs trip to the World Series the year before, Putnam's bypassed Lieb and engaged Brown to write the next team history in the series. In the realm of professional sports writing, a publisher's timetables are always linked to the fortunes of the ball club on the field. Completed manuscripts often languish for years in an editors' desk drawer or until someone decides that the moment is right—or until that so-called "magical season" spikes real-time fan interest. So it was for Brown and his Cubs book, which debuted in April 1947. It went through three reprintings before finally petering out.

Meanwhile, White Sox fans had little to savor during these dark years. Aside from the annual team-issued spring training press guides that rarely (if ever) reached the ticket-buying public, there had been only newspaper stories to look to for information about the Sox. No book about the American League team had been brought out since way back in 1919 when Gustav W. Axelson published a fawning biography of the "Old Roman," titled *Commy: The Life Story of Charles A. Comiskey*, for the Reilly & Lee Company in Chicago. That was it until 1952.

What good things could a prospective author contemplating this subject possibly begin to say about a team that had tossed away a World Series for the lure of the almighty dollar and then suffered through a three-decade malaise with no foreseeable end in sight? In order to stir the interest of Putnam's, or any other publisher, for that matter, a "Miracle on 35th Street" was sorely needed. Only then could this untold history finally reach its rightful audience.

World War II had shorn an already talent-thin ball club. The most recognizable stars, Luke Appling and Ted Lyons, were at or already past the age of forty. Luke and Teddy were returned to the opening-day roster in 1946 after marking time in the service of their country, but the losing ways went on as always through the bitter season of 1948 when the club finished dead last with 101 losses. In 1949 the White Sox scaled the heights and finished sixth but remained stuck in sixth place in 1950. However, a scent of a refreshing change hung in the air.

Baseball enjoyed a postwar popularity boom reflected in rising attendance figures, the lifting of the color barrier, and the restoration of the game's greatest stars to active duty. Inside the Comiskey Park inner sanctum at this time there occurred an important changing of the guard. Matriarch Grace Reidy Comiskey, widow of the "Old Roman" Charles Comiskey's son John Louis, elevated her son Charley to a full vice presidency and gave him a free hand to wheel and deal as he saw fit. Young Comiskey, a baseball tenderfoot at twenty-two years of age, played a surprisingly fine hand, as it turned out.

Unafraid to gamble on up-and-coming men of vision, however unproven, Comiskey spirited Frank Lane away from the Big Ten and told his new general manager to "go out and build me a ball club whatever the cost." Old gray heads in the baseball operation were let go, the farm system revitalized (with the first scout hired to identify and recruit top talent in the Negro Leagues), and a defeatist mindset that just getting by is good enough was swept away.

Lane in turn hired Paul Rapier Richards, a highly regarded Triple-A manager but untested at the big league level, to pilot the 1951 edition. This '51 team evolved into a team of legend, one remembered fondly for its daring base-stealing, "Go-Go" execution. Paul Richard's precision club inaugurated a new winning era and seventeen consecutive first-division finishes, a record equaled or surpassed by only the Yankees and Baltimore Orioles.

Blending the traditional strengths of strong pitching, speed, inner defense, and timely hitting minus the long ball, the White Sox were a national story in 1951. A fourteen-game winning streak from May 15 to 30 that year sealed the bargain and convinced Putnam's to move forward with a new book project for Warren Brown. *The Chicago White Sox* would be the eleventh in the series of team books, leaving only the Phillies, Senators, and woeful Browns without a publishing commitment.

An apocryphal tale, told to this writer in the early 1980s by the late Eddie Gold, a *Chicago Sun-Times* sportswriter of many years, reveals that the estimable Mr. Brown was said to have wagered the boys on the copy desk at the *Herald-American* that he could churn out a complete White Sox manuscript for Putnam's over the course of a single week-end. Whatever Warren's editor, Leo Fischer, might have said to him at that point is lost to history, but the point is moot. The boys back at the desk were said to have covered their bets, and the manuscript went off to press in the late fall of 1951.

From various resources, including team archives and the personal recollections drawn from the well-spring of Brown's fertile memory, the author produced an eminently readable 248-page hardcover tome rich in anecdote, wit, and insightful reminiscences. The book was published on Tuesday, April 1, 1952, thirteen days ahead of opening day.

In the promotional circulars touting the *The Chicago White Sox*, Brentano's Book Store at 29 S. Wabash Avenue promised "a complete history of the fabulous early days of the 'Old Roman' Charles A. Comiskey, the fateful and tragic years of his son J. Louis, and the behind-the-scenes tragedy of the Black Sox of 1919."

Indeed, there was no one more qualified to tell the story of this lamentable chapter of team history than Brown, who knew the Black Sox players intimately. "I still believe they were the greatest team that ever played baseball," he once said. His nuanced assessment of the White Sox in their darkest hour stops short of absolving the eight players of complicity to throw the World Series to Cincinnati, but Brown delivered a breakthrough account revealing for the first time the animus existing between the so-called "Clean Sox" loyal to Comiskey and the "Black Sox" contingent and the likelihood that they were conspiring to lose games in the heat of the 1920 flag chase as well. These points are crucial to our understanding of that pivotal episode in the fabric of early-twentieth-century urban history and American baseball. Latter-day historians including Eliot Asinof and Harold Seymour fail to cite Brown's original research in their own published volumes about the scandal.

The book officially debuted on April 12 at an autograph

signing at the old Mandel Brothers Department Store, with several of the 1952 team members on hand to lure in casual fans and the "walk-up" business. The knowledgeable and opinionated Brown had given Sox fans a scholarly but whimsical journey through the first five decades, but early reviews were mixed. *Chicago Tribune* columnist Will Leonard described his March 22, 1952, critique as a "review with a tape machine." "*The Chicago White Sox*, which will rank as the first definitive history of the South Siders[,] is interestingly apportioned: the Hitless Wonders of 1906 and their World Series victory over the Cubs are covered in four-and-a-half pages of the 248 pages. The scandalous 1919–1920 story fills 40," Leonard observed. "The entire decade of the '20s takes only 15. But the "Go-Go" saga of 1951 occupies 25 pages, more than any other single season in Hose history."

Of course it is always incumbent on an author of a baseball history to be cognizant of the publisher's promotional and marketing strategies and attach greater weight to the current team and the modern-day stars if only to entice the younger reader with no memory of earlier events to open the book. Early promotional advertising materials reinforced this point: "Without warning in 1951, the Chicago White Sox became the sensation of the sports world. They were the most interesting team to watch and according to astute baseball men, the most difficult to defeat. What can their admirers and their enemies, the other teams, expect in 1952?"

Regrettably, Mr. Brown was never allowed to answer that question in book form. He was not asked to provide an update to the first edition or carry the story forward through the exciting seasons that were to follow, culminating in the 1959 pennant. It was a first for the White Sox since 1919 and the climax to a "Go-Go" era that had dawned in 1951. The Putnam series wrapped up in 1955 with Fred Lieb's final volume covering the history of the St. Louis Browns/Baltimore Orioles.

Since the mid-1950s (apart from team-issued yearbooks and game programs), published volumes about the Chicago White Sox have been few and far between despite the team's greater success between the white lines than the cross-town Cubs, who have easily surpassed the South Siders in the published narrative despite a chronically poor record of achievement on the field. On average, since 1952, there have been five books written about the Cubs or the Wrigley Field environs to every new volume coming out about the up-and-down fortunes of the Sox.

In 1960, the late *Tribune* writer David Condon, mentored by Warren Brown early in his career, published a post–World Series wrap-up aptly titled *The Go-Go Chicago White Sox* for Coward-McCann, but it had a very short shelf life and gathers dust on library book shelves today. Eighteen years would pass before the next Sox book, my personal memoir of growing up a fan, titled *Stuck on the Sox*, found its way into print in the summer of 1978.

Sporadic White Sox books have followed, usually accompanying particularly memorable seasons or trips to the post-season in 1983, 1993, and, of course, in 2005, the entirely unexpected World Series Championship year: picture books, a *White Sox Encyclopedia*, several narratives of Nellie Fox and the 1959 season, two biographies of Minnie Minoso, the politics of stadium building in Chicago, a fan memoir by Richard Roeper, and a rather thin "day by day in Sox history" account from the early 1980s round out the White Sox canon. I suppose that is enough Sox books to fill at least *half* a shelf, or so I would hope.

This "new generation" of White Sox chroniclers, an inconspicuous but deeply passionate group of authors from varying backgrounds, find they cannot compete with the plethora of new books coming out each spring detailing the sagas of the fortunate few: the Red Sox, Yankees, and Cubs. But one thing is very certain: we all owe a tip of the cap to

Warren Brown, who set a standard we have strived to live up to in our musings about the team that we follow through thick and thin.

I was fortunate to acquire an inscribed copy of *The Chicago White Sox,* minus the dust jacket, from Patrick Quinn, Chicago's sports collector-hobbyist guru who sold it to me for a pittance in 1976. I rescued the cloth-bound book from the bottom of a box containing many other dog-eared, spine-cracked, out-of-print sports publications nobody wanted to buy.

"How much?" I asked Pat.

"Three bucks," he replied.

"Deal," I said. Later, in the car, as I drove away from his store on south Archer Avenue, I opened the book up and to my surprise and sheer delight I found the author's signature on the title page. That was two years before Warren Brown passed away. I can't help but believe that my signed first edition of *The Chicago White Sox* is worth a whole lot more today than three bucks. But who can attach a cash value to something like this? To me it is much more of a priceless heirloom, if only for the spiritual link it affords me to a trailblazing Hall of Fame pioneer of Chicago sports journalism who told the White Sox story with candor, honesty, wry humor, and style.

Richard C. Lindberg

ILLUSTRATIONS

THE CHICAGO WHITE SOX

CHAPTER ONE

ONE sunny summer's afternoon in 1876 a gangling, seventeen-year-old from Chicago's teeming West Side was making progress, such as it was, with a horse-drawn truckload of bricks destined for immediate use in reconstruction of the City Hall, a major project of the time. As his plodding span drew near Jackson and Laflin streets, the youth became aware of a ball game in progress between the Hatfields and the McCoys of Chicago's sandlot ranks. The youth, who had some pretensions as a pitcher, drew up his weary steeds and got down from the driver's seat for a more critical survey of the situation.

The Hatfields' pitcher was being clouted hither and yon by the rallying McCoys. Nobody was out. It didn't look as if anyone was ever going to get out. The frantic manager of the Hatfields was beside himself with rage at the bum deal the fates had given him. Soon he was standing beside the youth, lately descended from the load of bricks, who was now audibly voicing his own confident thought: "Gee! I can pitch better than that!"

In short order the youth, since he was not entirely unknown to the Hatfield's manager, was in there giving it a try. True enough he did do better than that. He stopped the rally. He stayed on the pitching job and the game went on and on. . . .

Meanwhile two miles or so to the northeast the city fathers, the sidewalk superintendents, and maybe even the trowel wielders themselves were wondering what had happened to that load of bricks, now long overdue. Leading the wonderment league was Honest John Comiskey, Alderman of the Seventh Ward and a Democratic Leader.

Now Honest John did not get to be an alderman and a leader without being a man of action. The other city fathers, the sidewalk superintendents, and the trowel wielders, good union men and true, might be content to wonder, but Honest John started out to find where in hell those bricks were. He followed the route the truck logically should have taken from the yard to the Hall and came eventually to Jackson and Laflin streets. There he found the load of bricks. Hard by, still busily engaged in baffling the erstwhile frisky McCoys, Honest John beheld his son, Charles, quondam driver of the truck.

Here again it was up to Honest John, the man of action. He had to make a decision, and make one quickly. Should he proceed forthwith to the center of the playing field and publicly take his son to task for letting down the city fathers and the Democratic party in their hour of need? Or should he mount to the driver's seat and get those bricks where they belonged without further delay?

Honest John made his choice. He took the bricks and drove away. He left his son committed to the game of baseball and thereby set in motion a train of the most interesting events the national pastime has ever recorded.

Charles A. Comiskey never again drove a truckload of bricks, not even for special delivery on the body and person of any member of the genus arbiter, or umpire, for which species the esteem of any ball player seldom lifts above .071 in the lifetime averages.

But if he had not paused in his last brick mission of 1876 there might not now be a Chicago White Sox organization. There might not now be an American League. The major leagues, as they are now known, would not have one and only one franchise whose fortunes have been continuously in the keeping of one family, that of Charles A. Comiskey and his descendants.

Certainly if the youth of seventeen had not alighted from his driver's seat that summer's day of 1876, abandoning the city fathers and their rebuilding program to their own resources, there would never have come a day in 1917 when their successors in the City Council would solemnly arise and unanimously pass the following resolution:

> WHEREAS our favorites, the White Sox, have won the pennant in the American League and with it the right to compete in series with the New York Giants for the baseball championship of the world, therefore be it
> RESOLVED that the City Council of the City of Chicago hereby extends its congratulations to Charles A. Comiskey and to the members of its baseball team for their splendid victory, and its best wishes that the White Sox may win further honors for themselves, their owner, and Chicago by showing New York's team that the "I Will" spirit is not to be denied.

From their very beginnings until the present, through the lifetime of Charles A. Comiskey and his son, J. Louis, right on down to the administration of his grandson, Charles A. Comiskey II, the Chicago White Sox have been an unpredictable organization.

They have taken in full stride the good, of which they have had ample share in the glorious past. They have not whimpered at the slings and arrows of outrageous fortune whose impact they have felt far more often than they have ever deserved.

Theirs is a real story of baseball's fun and sorrow, of bitter feuds and the clashing of forceful personalities. Theirs is the history of the Comiskey family, baseball's only dynasty.

Let us follow, then, the Comiskey trail from Jackson and Laflin streets to Thirty-fifth and Shields, though it take us, as indeed it must, to all parts of the United States, to Mexico, and on one never-to-be-forgotten junket clear around the world.

CHAPTER TWO

CHARLES A. COMISKEY's earliest attempts to practice his profession for pay, after the brick-truck episode, took him to Elgin, to Milwaukee, and in 1878 to Dubuque, where may be traced his first serious effort to attract attention to himself and his capabilities.

In Dubuque he came in contact with Ted Sullivan, who was to become a noted baseball organizer and founder of minor leagues, in the Middle West. From him the young Comiskey learned much that was to help him later on, when he was to double in the business as well as the playing phase of baseball.

Cast originally as a pitcher, Comiskey was also thrust into action as a third baseman, a first baseman, and an outfielder on days when his services were not needed in the box, for it was a well-manned squad indeed, in those early days of baseball, which boasted as many as ten or twelve players. They were in a sense baseball tyros with which Comiskey found himself associated. Yet one of them at Dubuque, also a pitcher, was Charles (Old Hoss) Radbourne, who five years later was to win sixty games for the Providence club, a record that has defied the onslaught of all the great pitchers who have come after him.

Comiskey's wages in those first few years ranged between fifty and sixty dollars a month, but in 1882 his development had reached such a point that he attracted the attention of the St. Louis Browns of the American Association. Their attractive offer of $125 a month gained for them a man who was to revolutionize first-base play.

It was while holding forth for the Browns that the imaginative Comiskey decided to apply the principles of the man in motion to the first-base job. Until then it was common practice for the guardian of that spot to keep his foot anchored to the base. Comiskey ranged afield, moved back from the base and over into the territory between him and the second baseman.

This radical move created a sensation at the time, and before long all first basemen were doing it, and a job which had been suitable for the lumbering, sedentary type of athlete now called for players of agility.

Comiskey caught the fancy of the St. Louis fans and the club's ownership to such an extent that at the end of the 1883 season he was made manager.

The American Association with which St. Louis was identified was in reality no more than a sectional circuit. It had no such claims to wide territorial range in its member cities as did the National League, which had come into existence in 1876 one year before Comiskey made his swap of bricks for baseball.

However, by the end of the 1885 season, Comiskey's second in charge of the Browns, his club won the pennant in the Association. No. 1 team in the National League was Adrian C. Anson's Chicago team, forerunners of the Cubs.

They were a formidable team, at the time generally acknowledged to be the best in professional baseball. Comiskey thought otherwise. His challenge to Anson's team was accepted, and in a series that endured through seven games, there was glory and disappointment for both. The series ended with each having won three games, and one was a tie.

Since nothing was proved this time, they tried it again when both occupied the top of their respective leagues in the following season. This time Comiskey's Browns took the series, four games to two, and the Chicago National League club felt for the first time the spell of a Comiskey opponent, which it never has been able to shake.

The St. Louis Browns, under Comiskey's direction, gained championships in 1887 and again in 1888, but were unsuccessful in their postseason skirmishing in 1887 with Detroit, and the following year with New York.

The St. Louis–Detroit series ranged through fifteen games, and when it finished, after a tour of practically the entire known baseball world, Detroit had won ten and St. Louis five. In the New York series the Browns finished on the short end of a six-to-four count of the games played.

Comiskey remained with St. Louis through the 1889 season. At the end of the season, he cast his lot with the downtrodden and oppressed players who were dissatisfied with the current wage scale. The outcome of all this was the organization of the Players or Brotherhood League, which lasted through the season of 1890.

During that year, Comiskey had charge of the team that was placed in Chicago. There is no doubt but that his burning desire to head a baseball team in his home town and make a success of it moved him every bit as much as any craving to put organized ownership and management in its proper place. However, the time was not yet at hand when Comiskey could take his place as a commanding figure in Chicago baseball. His first venture was a monumental bust, and sadder and wiser, he returned to St. Louis in 1891.

He was not to remain there very long. The following year he was attracted to Cincinnati, where he joined the Reds as manager. His activity with the Cincinnati club through three seasons made no lasting mark on baseball, but his stay there, and an association and friendship he made with the thirty-dollar-a-month sports editor of the *Commercial-Gazette* was indeed a milestone in baseball history.

The young sports editor was Byron Bancroft Johnson, and as a result of the efforts of these two there was to arise the American League as it is now constituted.

The American Association was beginning to come apart at the seams, and Comiskey thought it would be possible to reorganize its more profitable clubs and out of them establish an organization to be known as the Western League. It was also his idea that the man best qualified to head this circuit was Ban Johnson.

It took some selling on Comiskey's part, for even in his young days Johnson was a man of sharp likes and dislikes. Those who knew him were either for him or against him. There was no middle course, and Johnson, outspoken, irascible, and ever ready for a fight or a frolic didn't care much, one way or another.

When Comiskey put his man over, it was logical that he should go right along with him. The remains of the Sioux City Club were acquired, and Comiskey, with Johnson's blessing, moved the franchise to St. Paul.

The National League, the one recognized major organization, was lumbering along with an unwieldy dozen clubs, while the more compact eight-club Western League was gradually gaining confidence in its own future, driven as it was by Johnson, the power seeker, and Comiskey, who lived for the day when he could re-establish himself in his home town, Chicago.

Toward the end of the 1899 season Comiskey and Johnson thought the time was at hand for the grand entry.

The owner of the Chicago National League club was James A. Hart, who strenuously opposed the entry of another club, even one of minor-league status, into Chicago. Johnson and Comiskey would not take no for an answer. They pressed the point so vehemently that the National League was moved to take up the matter at a special meeting in Cleveland.

Present, among others, were Hart and John T. Brush, the owner of the Cincinnati club, who never had cared very much for Johnson, first as a sports writer critical of the Brush regime, and afterward as an upstart president of a minor league. However, before the meeting adjourned, permission was given Johnson and Comiskey to put a club in Chicago, though the restrictions were such that it was a case of the ambitious Western Leaguers taking it and liking it.

Comiskey's St. Paul organization, therefore, moved into Chicago, although the National League had specified that wherever the new club lit, it must not come farther north than Thirty-fifth Street. Furthermore, the Chicago National League club was to have the right to draft players from the Western League invader.

With Chicago as its principal city, the newly arranged league now included Buffalo, Cleveland, Detroit, Indianapolis, Milwaukee, Minneapolis, and Kansas City. Seven of these cities no doubt were important enough in their way, but the one fact which had bearing on the entire future of major-league baseball was that Comiskey was back in Chicago with a ball club—this time to stay.

CHAPTER THREE

WHILE the National League, much against its will, had ungraciously yielded the Western League (now called the American League) permission to enter Chicago, it went right on pretending that baseball had but one major organization. Drafting of players from the American League was unrestricted.

The Chicago Nationals reached into the Kansas City club and for $500 drafted Jimmy Callahan, along with four other players. The American League, with the fiery Johnson protesting all the way, did not fancy this ruthless treatment of its property but was unable to do much about it for the first year of its existence.

The new league went through its first season, and its winner was Comiskey's Chicago club, which won eighty-two and lost fifty-three for a .607 percentage. At the season's end the club was ahead of runner-up Milwaukee by a four-game margin.

Confident in its own future, the American League now began to make demands rather than polite requests, and a baseball war was speedily in the making.

The National League's overstuffed membership was being pared, and when such cities as Baltimore and Washington were abandoned, Johnson proposed to take them into his league. The National League didn't care too much for that, but Johnson went right along with his plans. He was fighting an offensive war now. His league had prospects. It had money. It was ready for a fight to the finish.

Comiskey touched off a real bombshell when he induced Callahan and Clark Griffith to jump the Chicago Nationals and join up with the White Sox. That nickname had now been adopted by Comiskey's team, after having been in disuse for many seasons. It orginated with "Pop" Anson's National League club at an earlier stage of Chicago's baseball history.

Griffith, a great pitcher of his time, was also made manager of the White Sox, Comiskey being content with his activity as owner not only of his own club, but with Johnson co-organizer of the league itself. Buffalo had been replaced with Boston. A newly created Philadelphia franchise was turned over to Connie Mack, who had been at Milwaukee. The latter city retained its franchise through 1901.

A third figure, and an important one in the stabilizing of the American League, was Charles W. Somers, owner of the Cleveland club. It was he who was induced by Johnson to finance the new operations in Philadelphia. When Mack took charge there, an option to purchase the property, shortly exercised, was given to Ben Shibe.

In the considerably reorganized circuit, the White Sox were again champions, this time with eighty-three won and fifty-three lost for a .610 record. Griffith was as efficient a pitcher as he was a manager, for his twenty-four victories and seven defeats led the league's hurlers.

Griffith continued to manage the White Sox through the 1902 season, but the best the club could do was fourth, the championship going to Mack's Philadelphia team. The season was notable for a no-hit, no-run game turned in by Callahan against Detroit on September 20. Notable, that is, for White Sox records, since this same Callahan before his course was run was to figure in many an adventure with Comiskey's team.

The league itself, still in the process of being molded nearer President Johnson's heart's desire, had transferred the Milwaukee franchise to St. Louis, at Comiskey's urging. The White Sox owner had not forgotten his own interesting experiences in the Mound City over an eight-year span in the eighties.

This left Baltimore and its famous Orioles as the one franchise not destined to remain in existence as one of the American League's solid eight. However, it required some very undiplomatic processes to dislodge Baltimore. The first batch of these was delivered in the midst of the 1902 season.

For the proper appreciation of the strange machinations about to take place, it will have to be recalled that John T. Brush, the Cincinnati owner in the nineties, cherished an undying dislike for Ban Johnson and all his works. Brush, by 1902, was serving as chairman of the National League executive committee, though he was then considering dealing the Cincinnati property to August Herrmann. He was looking toward New York, where owner Andy Freedman's tactics had prevented any immediate peace in the player-raiding warfare the American League was waging against the older circuit.

In July, 1902, John McGraw of the Baltimore Orioles and owner of a block of stock in the club, sold it to John J. Mahon, then president of the club, and jumped to the New York Giants. Within a week Mahon's holdings were sold to Brush for $15,000, the sum being prorated among the National League clubs.

Here, indeed, was a weird situation. The National League, which Johnson was fighting so bitterly, was now owner of the majority stock in one of the American League clubs. As owners, the Nationals straightway instructed Baltimore players Joe McGinnity, Roger Bresnahan, Dan McGann, and one other to report to McGraw at New York. Players Cy Seymour and Joe Kelley were dispatched to the Cincinnati Reds. Thus Brush calculated a death blow would be struck to the American League and Johnson's plans. But Brush had merely succeeded in outwitting himself.

The wholesale departure of players, followed by the injury of others, brought about a situation wherein Baltimore was unable to field a team against St. Louis, July 17, and forfeited the game. By American League rules of procedure, the Baltimore franchise was forfeited and reverted to the American League—which left Brush and his associates holding a $15,000 bag that was actually not worth fifteen cents.

Once in possession of the Baltimore franchise, Johnson was able to restock it with players borrowed from other clubs in the American League and finish out the season.

While Brush was reeling from this blow to his bank roll, Johnson arrived in New York breathing fire and brimstone. Manhattan had not yet encountered a character such as the forceful American League president. He took every advantage of what he called the treachery of his erstwhile associates, Brush and McGraw, to secure both a sympathetic audience for his story, and backing for his project.

His project, incidentally, was breath-taking, for Byron Bancroft Johnson proposed to invade New York itself and place therein the franchise lately taken from Baltimore. This, indeed, was the war to a finish that Johnson and Comiskey had plotted when they were snubbed once too often by the older league.

On his side Johnson had right, or so he insisted, long and loudly. He had adequate financial backing. He had the gift of promotional projection of himself and his interests as has been seldom given to a baseball executive. He broke down the last defense of the once proud National League, and in a meeting at Cincinnati, January 10, 1903, baseball peace was declared. New York was in the American League, and the American League was on a par with the National, a major organization.

Where, you will say, did the fortunes of Comiskey and the White Sox figure in all this?

The New York American League club's first manager was Clark Griffith, dispatched there by Comiskey. Replacing him as field leader of the White Sox was Callahan, who had jumped with Griff from the Chicago Nationals when the first sound of heavy firing was discernible in the baseball war.

CHAPTER FOUR

THE BALL PARK in which the White Sox had been plying their trade since the invasion of Chicago in 1900 was the site of the old Chicago Cricket Club grounds at Thirty-ninth and Princeton Avenue. It had been selected by Comiskey and Ban Johnson, who came to Chicago with no great amount of capital but with utmost confidence in their own productive abilities.

The story is told that they repaired to the Foreman Bank for a loan and were asked what they had in the way of collateral. "Only our good names," they confessed, but the bank president must have been a baseball fan at heart. They got what money they needed to whip the field into shape so that baseball of sorts might be played in early April, 1900.

It was partly on this ground and partly on the Cubs' West Side playing field that Callahan, third in the series of White Sox managers, directed his American League seventh-place team in the 1903 post-season series with the Cubs. This was a memorable set of games. It progressed through fourteen, with each side having won seven, before the Cub manager, Frank Selee, called a halt. Comiskey and Callahan wanted to continue, at least into the fifteenth game that a decision might be reached, but Selee protested that it had lasted so long now the Cub player contracts had expired—and besides, Joe Tinker, the Cubs' great shortstop, really had to get to Kansas City, object matrimony.

The 1904 season was preceded by a training trip to Marlin Springs, Texas. Among those who showed up for survey that spring was Ed Walsh, a young and handsome pitcher, who had been drafted from Newark. Walsh was fully aware of his good looks, but the only impression he made on Comiskey and Callahan was that of a burly right hander who had terrific speed but no control, and who was a complete flop as a fielder of bunts and such other chances as ordinarily come the way of a pitcher. Walsh, for most of the training time, meant very little in the White Sox plans for the season, or for the future, and, as a result, he was left largely to his own devices.

While going through the motions of training, Walsh became aware of a pitch that was being thrown by Elmer Stricklett, who had been around and about baseball for some time. Stricklett said he had learned the pitch from one Corridon, in the employ of the Philadelphia Nationals. It consisted of wetting two of the fingers and applying them to the baseball, prior to letting it go. This was the "spitball" whose quaint swerves from the straight and narrow were to baffle many a batsman. It was also to lead to a great variety of other freak pitches, such as the "mud ball," the "emery ball," and the "shine ball," until the baseball-powers-that-be in their wisdom ruled out all freak pitches in 1920, though permitting those exponents of the spitter still employed in the American and National Leagues to finish out their careers without abandoning it as their stock in trade.

Walsh was intrigued by the queer quirks a baseball could take as demonstrated by Stricklett. He resolved to

18

adopt the pitch as his own, and spent long hours mastering its delivery. He was to become, in time, its greatest exponent in baseball. Stricklett, who taught him the pitch, became a victim of a sore arm and left the White Sox without ever having contributed anything to its records.

The sore arm, which shortened Stricklett's career, was supposed to be an occupational disease with spitball pitchers, though baseball records contain many names, both in major and minor leagues, to argue that this isn't necessarily so. Jack Chesbro, Burleigh Grimes, Urban Faber, Clarence Mitchell, who was left handed to boot, Walsh himself, and Frank Shellenback are some of those who ended their active days as pitchers only because of advancing years, and not because of any arm ailment brought about by addiction to the spitter.

Parenthetically, twenty years after Walsh first encountered the pitch at Marlin Springs, he was serving as a coach for the White Sox in their spring camp at Winter Haven, Florida. At the instance of some curious baseball reporters who wanted to know if he could still throw a spitter, Walsh, the supremely confident showman to the last, said he could. In the Florida sunshine he warmed up carefully and then declared he was ready. For several minutes, or until the curiosity of his inquisitors was satisfied, he gave a demonstration of the spitball's mastery that would certainly have baffled such hitters as the White Sox had in camp at the time, or baffled them as long as Walsh's condition would permit him to throw against them.

Walsh remained with the White Sox squad when it made its way north in 1904. However, he was not yet quite ready to take his place with the pitching staff that was to reach championship stature two years later. Nor was the club itself, though Comiskey, now that he had no more baseball wars to fight, was impatient to get together as quickly as possible his first major-league championship team.

19

The pennants he had won as a manager at St. Louis in the old American Association, and the ones he and Griffith acquired in the first two years of the new league were important enough in their place, but this was a major league in which Comiskey was now concerned. He was in the big league. He wanted a winner.

If Walsh wasn't yet able to help him to that goal in 1904, there was another pitcher on the payroll, the left-hander, G. Harris (Doc) White, who measured up. In September, starting with his game on the twelfth, Doc White began a string of shutouts that endured through five successive games.

In midseason of 1904, the White Sox were subjected to another change in managers, their fourth. Callahan abandoned organized baseball pursuits for the time being, and the job of leadership was turned over to Fielder Jones, who was a charter member of the White Sox, along with Billy Sullivan, the catcher, Frank Isbell, and Roy Patterson, pitcher. Jones, an outfielder, remained as a playing manager, which was more the rule than the exception in baseball at the time.

The combined Callahan-Jones management lifted the White Sox to a respectable third-place finish in 1904, and the following season they moved a space nearer the top, finishing second behind Connie Mack's Philadelphia team, winning ninety-two and losing sixty for a .605 average.

Among the games they won was a 15 to 0 triumph of Frank Smith over Detroit. In it the Tigers were held hitless as Smith demonstrated that he was ready to do his pitching share to bring Comiskey his first American League pennant.

Twenty-four of the White Sox victories in 1905 were the property of Nick Altrock. He was then a much more serious-minded left-handed artisan than might have been suspected in later years, when as a coach of the Washington

20

club he was one of baseball's most storied cutups. Altrock had been discarded by Boston in 1903 and caught on with the White Sox. He turned in nineteen victories in his full season of 1904, but had dropped fourteen other verdicts along the way. The 1905 season was his best as a major-league pitcher, but in 1906 he was an able mate of Walsh, White, Frank Owen, and Smith, when the pennant for which Comiskey yearned came his way at last.

CHAPTER FIVE

FIELDER JONES directed these White Sox of 1906 to ninty-three won and fifty-eight lost for a .616 finish and their first American League championship. They gained it despite the unbelievably low combined batting average of .228 for the season, for they were the "Hitless Wonders."

It would be nice to say that their victory, the first under the Comiskey banner, set Chicago by the ears. But it wouldn't be strictly true. In that same season, Frank Chance, the Peerless Leader, was guiding the Chicago Cubs to a National League championship. In so doing he was setting up a record of one-hundred-sixteen games won and but thirty-six lost for a .763 percentage, a seasonal record that has been threatened seriously only once when the great New York Yankees of 1927 won one-hundred-ten games.

This was the Cub team which featured Tinker and Evers and Chance, which had the great pitching staff of Brown and Reulbach, of Pfiester, Lundgren, and Overall.

It was the team over which all Chicago, save the dissenting South Siders, raved and ranted. It was baseball's best. It was too bad that lovable Charlie Comiskey, now that he had satisfied his life's ambition and had gained a major-league pennant, would have to face these man-eaters of the National League, and be destroyed.

To make matters worse for the White Sox, George Davis, their regular shortstop, had been injured prior to the series. This caused Manager Jones to move Lee Tannehill from third to short. It brought into the series the inexperienced and little known George Rohe, at third base.

The world's series, that is the meeting of American and National League champions, had been started in 1903 when Jimmy Collins' Boston American League team defeated Fred Clarke's Pittsburgh National League team, five games to three. There was no series in 1904, but in 1905 John McGraw's Giants defeated Connie Mack's Athletics, four games to one. The 1906 series was therefore the first in history when both championship teams represented the same city.

It was the unheralded sub, Rohe, whose triple off Mordecai Brown broke up the first game, played at the Cubs' park on the West Side. The score was 2 to 1. Apart from Rohe's potent thrust there hadn't been much to choose between the resistance Brown and Nick Altrock, the White Sox pitcher, offered to the attack of rival batsmen.

Four hits were all each side made. For all practical purposes, Chance's high and mighty Cubs were as much "Hitless Wonders" as the White Sox, who were more used to such meager batting fare. Only in the matter of strikeouts did Brown and Altrock differ in other pitching records. The Miner fanned seven to Nick's three. Each walked one, each made one wild pitch, and each allowed four hits, but the lone extra-base hit and the ball game was Rohe's.

The next day the traffic moved to the White Sox park. In its setting Ed Reulbach turned in his memorable one-hit effort, which was to stand alone in world's series pitching annals until another Cub, Claude Passeau, came along in 1945 against the Detroit Tigers and equaled it.

The lone White Sox hit belonged to Jiggs Donohue, the flashy first baseman. Under the circumstances, there wasn't much the Comiskey clan could do about winning the ball game. It went to the Cubs, 7 to 1. Chance's wrecking crew piled up a ten-hit total off Doc White and Frank Owen, and further enjoyed themselves to the extent of stealing five bases.

Chicago's baseball fandom was reasonably certain after this display that the Cubs were not going to be denied now, and would make short work of the American League upstarts. But the Cubs hadn't seen anything of Ed Walsh, or all of Rohe, as yet. They had put down Rohe's opening game winning triple as one of those things that might happen to anyone. They were a bit wrong on that.

Chance had his left-hander, Jack Pfiester, ready for the return to the West Side grounds. Pfiester responded with a four hitter. Unfortunately for his cause one of them was another triple by Rohe, which took care of the ball game, then and there. This one the White Sox won, 3 to 0, the shutout being a natural consequence of the pitching Walsh was doing. He held the Cubs to two hits, a double by Frank Schulte and Arthur Hofman's single. He struck out twelve. He walked but one. Since the Cubs weren't getting on base, they were no menace to White Sox catcher Billy Sullivan's throwing arm in this game. But just for the hell of it, Rohe, the now famous added starter, swiped the game's only base, to the chagrin of wily Johnny Kling, the Cubs' catcher.

Back to the White Sox park went the big show for the next day. By now it was understood by one and all that the mighty Cubs had picked on an opponent that was rapidly cutting them down to size.

The fourth game saw the largest attendance so far re-

Ed Walsh, one of the White Sox greatest pitchers who in 1908 won 40 games, 12 of them shutouts. (*The Sporting News.*)

Fielder Jones, manager of the White Sox, 1904-1906, whose "Hitless Wonders" won the world's championship in 1906. (*The Sporting News.*)

corded in the series, with 18,385 present when Miner Brown came through with a magnificent two-hit performance to win, 1 to 0, and square the series.

Altrock, victor in the first game, again opposed Brownie, and Nick did quite well, if not well enough. He ran afoul of Chance, the manager, who not only could lead but was not above dragging his team to victory when the need arose. (A sort of 1906 model of Lou Boudreau, Cleveland's heroic 1948 force-of-example manager.) It was on one of his two hits off Altrock that Chance made his way around the bases in the seventh to score the game's only run.

Until now the games had been completely under control of the pitchers, but in the fifth, and next to closing engagement of the series, the hitters escaped from the spell.

Walsh was cuffed for three runs in the first inning, and Reulbach yielded one. The White Sox master of the spitball righted himself and went along more steadily until the seventh inning when he was removed as a precautionary measure, with Doc White finishing up.

By that time Reulbach had been driven to cover. So had Pfiester, and Orval Overall was in charge of a losing 8 to 6 venture. That was the final score of the game, which found the White Sox gathering twelve hits from assorted Cub pitching. Frank Isbell, a silent partner through the first four games, broke out in this game with a rash of four two-base hits.

Glorying in their new found batting ability, the White Sox moved for the kill in the closing number at their own park the next day.

They began with a rush against Brown, knocking him out in less than two innings, during which they racked up seven runs. For the balance of the game they were content with six hits and another run off Overall, but the seven run—eight hit attack that had routed Brown, the

Cubs' pride and joy, in the second inning was more than enough to insure the onetime "Hitless Wonders" the game and championship. Doc White, working steadily all the way, scattered seven hits among the Cubs and well earned his 8 to 3 victory.

So elated was Comiskey over his first world's championship, he threw his share of the first four games' receipts into the players' pool. Just what Comiskey's contribution to the pool was is uncertain. There was no detailed breakdown of baseball's financial items in 1906 as was to become a "must" in later years. The players' pool was $33,401.70, each club took $31,246.65 and the Commission took $10,655 out of the receipts for the six games.

Since the players' pool took the major share of the first four games, Comiskey's end could not have been very large. The club owners did not start collecting in earnest until after four games were played. Some latter day statisticians place Comiskey's contribution to the players' pool at approximately $6,000. Others put the figure nearer $12,000. Whatever it was, Comiskey was to learn soon that his turning it over to the players was a tactical error.

CHAPTER SIX

In the pursuance of any lengthy discussion of the Comiskey dynasty's baseball fortunes, the way of a Comiskey with a dollar is an inescapable topic. For that reason, the first brush of the "Old Roman" and his legions over the matter of finances is as pertinent to the story as some economic problems of later years which were given much wider attention.

It was his habit to award his players with bonuses after they had done something, rather than before. In this aid to inspiration he was followed somewhat, many years later, when P. K. Wrigley, owner of the Cubs, evolved his "basic-salary" plan. This presumed to reward players in season for what they were doing that was for the greater good of the club. It was too complicated for the mentalities of the players who were then serving Wrigley and was abandoned, with the Cubs reverting to the more familiar process of rewarding a player by a salary raise for the next season, for something he had done in the last.

When Comiskey threw his share into the world's series pot of 1906 and added it to the players' total, which broke down to $1,874.01 as each winning Sox share, he felt that he was showing practical appreciation. But when it came time to talk contract with the players for the 1907 season, he discovered to his dismay that many of his men had figured the world's series share, their own and Comiskey's, as a normal part of the 1906 season. This they added to whatever sums their 1906 season contracts had called for, and the total was their idea of the "basic" salary from which to start 1907 negotiations.

Comiskey's idea, from the start, was to pay a player what he judged him to be worth. He would resist to the end any holdout campaign a player launched and then, perversely, when the player had surrendered, Comiskey like as not would ink into the contract the figures first specified by the player. The worth of the player, in Comiskey's own judgment, was ever the determining factor in his wage, however. He was to say, when Babe Ruth was striding across the land as a player whose annual salary had reached hitherto unscaled heights: "Because Babe Ruth is worth $50,000 a year, it doesn't make $1,500 bushers worth $12,000."

In the months between the winning of his first world's championship and the start of the next season's campaign, Comiskey's difficulties with his players over their salaries were not enough to keep him from taking the White Sox to Mexico City to train. No one before him had ever attempted anything like it, and no one was sure whether anyone that deep in Mexico knew anything of baseball or cared. The White Sox made the trip, and emerged safely. If their visit set up an interest in the game that was one day to cause some of Mexico's citizens to raid the major leagues for playing talent, perhaps that, too, can be blamed on Comiskey.

When the White Sox, champions of all they surveyed in the United States as well as Mexico, returned to the business of the American League, they were not quite up to duplicating their previous season's record. They finished third in a race which was won by Detroit. Though the world's championship remained in Chicago that year, it belonged to Chance's Cubs, who had recovered from the indignities heaped upon them by the "Hitless Wonders" twelve months before.

In the matter of individual performance the White Sox had something to offer this season. Their first baseman, Jiggs Donohue, completed his year with 1,986 chances, 1,846 being put-outs. Both of these are first basemen defensive marks that have been undisturbed since. Walsh, the once impossible fielder in the Marlin training camp, set a league record with 227 assists and 262 chances accepted. In one game he handled thirteen chances, and twice that season he recorded eleven assists in a game. Doc White worked sixty-five and one-third consecutive innings through August and September during which he did not issue a single base on balls.

The 1908 season, which was to be the last in which Fielder Jones figured as the White Sox manager, came very close to being another in which Chicago would wind up with a world's series all its own, since the Cubs went on to win again. On the very last day of the season, the Detroit Tigers beat the White Sox in a game that settled the championship. It also partly settled Jones' managerial career, though the immediate cause was not that his team had blown the pay-off game, but rather some of the circumstances leading up to it and some that followed.

Frank Smith, who had one no hitter to his credit earlier in his White Sox career, came through with another when he defeated Philadelphia, 1 to 0, in late September. But Smith had gone through a session in the Jones' "doghouse" in this season, when he stood indefinitely suspended as a result of what seemed to the manager to be a minor pitching indiscretion at the time. It had consisted of wasting a couple of pitches when there seemed to be no reason for it. Jones did not take the pitcher to task, but later the manager was questioned by Comiskey about the incident. Comiskey left Jones with the distinct impression that he would be a better manager if he were firm with his men. By making an example of one of them, no matter how important the individual might be, if the occasion warranted it, the greater good of the White Sox would be served. After thinking that over, Jones put Smith in the "doghouse," and not until near the end of the season was the door opened and Smith let out.

Even a Class D second guesser needed no time to figure out that a pitcher of Smith's undenied talents couldn't have helped but win a game somewhere along the line when his services were denied by managerial order—and that one game would have been enough to keep the Tigers from crashing through on the season's final day.

For the decisive game Jones selected Doc White as his pitcher. He was badly off form, and Ed Walsh, hastily rushed to the rescue, wasn't much better. Jones' third choice was Smith and at no time in his career was the pitcher more effective, but the game had gone down the drain by this time.

In the post-mortem of the season, Jones argued that he had made the proper move. White was invariably effective against the Tigers, and Walsh—well, Big Ed was then finishing up as great a season as he or any other pitcher ever enjoyed. In the course of it the master of the spitball had worked sixty-six games. He had pitched 464 innings. Both were (and still are) record performances for the league.

On September 29 in a double-header he had beaten Boston 5 to 1, and 2 to 0, allowing three hits in one game, four in another. He led the league with forty victories and fifteen defeats, and all this for a seasonal wage of $3,500, a like sum being promptly handed to him as a bonus by Comiskey at the end of the season.

Nor was that Walsh's only activity of 1908 worthy of being included in the White Sox history. On October 2 he encountered Cleveland, with Addie Joss as his opponent, and held the Indians to one run. Normally, even the light-hitting White Sox might have won for Big Ed on that basis, but this was the day on which Joss was to gain pitching immortality by turning the White Sox back without hit or run, permitting no man to get to first base—a "perfect game," no less, but in 1908 it took something like that to beat Big Ed Walsh.

These 1908 White Sox, working under Fielder Jones' direction for the last time, were able to establish another record peculiarly their own in the course of the season.

As a team they produced exactly three home runs in 156 games, the fewest ever hit by a major-league club.

True, the home run wasn't the ordinary occurrence it has come to be since the Ruth era, and Sam Crawford of the Tigers led the American League that year with a quota of seven. But three for an entire club in 156 games was cutting it rather thin.

All of these things no doubt contributed to some extent to the departure of Jones from the managerial seat, but the real cause was Fielder's ambition. Comiskey had heard some rumblings of his manager's dissatisfaction and sent for him.

"Name your terms," said Comiskey, "and I'll give you a contract for as long as you care to stay."

"I want a partnership, or nothing," was Jones' ultimatum.

It was nothing, for the Comiskey dynasty then and thereafter was a closed corporation, admitting none to partnership who weren't of the blood.

CHAPTER SEVEN

THE Comiskey policy of selecting a manager from the ranks continued after the departure of Jones. Billy Sullivan, the catcher, who had been with the club when it made its Chicago debut, was placed in charge. He lasted through the 1909 season, during which the club was barely able to lift its head above the .500 mark and finished in fourth place, the championship once more going to Detroit.

Though he was as interested in the performance of his players as ever, Comiskey had something of even greater importance in mind during 1909. He wanted a real major-league ball park, one that would stand as a monument to the Comiskey dynasty.

Work on the project began in the fall of 1909 and went on through the winter and into the spring of 1910, for which season Comiskey for the first time went out of the ranks to get the White Sox a field manager. His choice was Hugh Duffy, whose .438 batting average with the Boston Nationals through 124 games in 1894 still stands as a baseball record.

With Duffy in charge, the White Sox formally opened their new park at Thirty-fifth and Shields Avenue, on July 1, 1910, and were hosts to a crowd of 24,000. The new park, following out playing-field plans formulated by Comiskey, was symmetrical. In its first stages each foul line extended 362 feet. The distance to dead center was 420 feet. The symmetry of the playing surface is still maintained, though some of the distances are shorter as the park now stands.

It was Comiskey's idea that high-class baseball could be played only in a park in which anything a batsman made he earned, and one on which a fielder had room to roam. Comiskey Park, though rebuilt since 1910, still gives that impression. Its foul lines now extend 352 feet and the bleachers in center field, 440 feet away, have resisted the attack of all hitters save Hank Greenberg and Jimmy Foxx.

There was a time in the 1930's when Comiskey Park made its one concession to a hitter of its own, a practice which is common in other baseball enclosures in both major leagues. Indeed, the trick fences set up in recent years to aid and abet "distance" hitting production by the home guard have been the rule, rather than the exception.

The White Sox did it when their distant barriers baffled Al Simmons. The home plate was moved out a bit, so that in the redesigning of the field, the left- and right-field foul lines extended but 348 feet.

For the grand opening in 1910 Comiskey Park had a single-deck grandstand of concrete and steel, with bleachers and a pavilion of wood. This structure was adequate for the club's needs until 1926, when double-deck stands were constructed, extending all the way around left and right field and leaving a small bleacher section in center. This tremendous construction task, involving an expenditure of almost $1,000,000, gave Comiskey Park its present capacity of 53,000. An equivalent sum, various estimates say, had been expended in the park by the time it was opened in 1910.

Now that he had a park, it was Comiskey's earnest wish

to get together a ball club worthy of it. The one he had in 1910 was hardly that. It did merit some consideration in any review of White Sox teams, however. It went through 156 games with a team batting average of .212, sixteen points lower than the batting depths to which the "Hitless Wonders" of 1906 had sunk.

It was a sixth-place team, and when it rose no higher than fourth, a change in managers was indicated. For the seventh White Sox manager in the twelve years of the club's existence, Comiskey chose to try a repeater. He sent for Jimmy Callahan, who had been occupied since leaving the club in 1904 running a profitable semipro club known as the Logan Squares.

Callahan had long since abandoned his pitching, and was now an accomplished outfielder. When he returned to the White Sox he brought in as one of his coaches, William (Kid) Gleason, a scrappy little soul, who was one day going to be involved in the most dismaying set of circumstances that ever confronted a major-league ball club.

The White Sox of this particular time were very much in a state of flux. Most of the players who had attained championship stature in 1906 and just missed it in 1908 were passing on, and in 1910 the team wound up sixth, out of the first division for the first time since 1903. An effort was made to rebuild, but, then, as now that was a complicated process. However, the Callahan shake-up did lift the team to fourth for two seasons. The newcomers were yet to prove sensations though there were two who came in for the 1913 season who were to leave an indelible mark on baseball history's pages.

One of these was a small-sized catcher, Ray Schalk, who had been obtained from Milwaukee for $18,000. The other was a shortstop, George (Buck) Weaver, who had been

Urban "Red" Faber, one of the Sox most durable and reliable pitchers in the early days. (*The Sporting News.*)

Charles A. Comiskey, founder and first president of the Chicago White
Sox. (*The Sporting News.*)

planted by the White Sox in San Francisco, and then recalled.

Still more or less active in the White Sox pitching corps was Big Ed Walsh, and he sniffed at the sight of the pint-sized Schalk, audibly wondering how this rookie would ever be able to handle the mystifying Walsh spitball.

"Warm up, you big fathead, and I'll show you," invited Schalk. And proceeded to do so, handling Walsh's delivery with ease and efficiency. For the balance of his stay with the White Sox Walsh would not permit anyone else but Schalk to be his catcher.

Weaver, at first an erratic fielder given to throwing baseballs well away from their target, had been consigned to San Francisco for the purpose of gaining control.

Danny Long, the San Francisco manager, and a White Sox friend and fancier, was instructed to keep Weaver in the ball games, though he did make life miserable for the cluster of fans in the stand behind first base. In those days, contrary to present standards, minor-league clubs were willing to go along as correctors of weaknesses in men sent down by the major leagues. Nowadays, the minor-league clubs are committed to a policy of winning pennants in their own set, and rarely are willing to serve as a means of polishing up farmed-out talent, especially if the farmed out talent is apt to blow a few ball games, while attaining the proper sheen.

The 1912 and 1913 seasons, which were in reality the beginning of the White Sox long haul to an other world's championship, presented yet another of Comiskey's promotional bids for recognition, this time not only in the major leagues but all the way around the world.

At the conclusion of the 1912 season, in which the White Sox finished fourth, a joint meeting of the major leagues took place in Chicago. Following one of its sessions, Comiskey and one of his closest friends and confidants, Joe

Farrell, paid a visit to Smiley Corbett's bar, a favorite rendezvous for the sporting gentry.

Present when Comiskey arrived were John McGraw and Garry Hermann, and one thing led to another. Someone recalled that it had been twenty-five years since A. G. Spalding and Pop Anson had taken a team of baseball players around the world.

"That's something I'd like to do," said Comiskey.

"Me, too," said McGraw.

"Let's," said Comiskey.

They shook hands on it—and quite unlike most barroom pacts, did not forget about it, though it was not until a year later that the tour got underway.

CHAPTER EIGHT

THE personally conducted Comiskey-McGraw trip around the world left America's shores on November 19, 1913, when the party sailed for Vancouver. By that time the "White Sox" and the "Giants" as they were called (chiefly because Comiskey and his manager, Jimmy Callahan, headed one, and McGraw the other) were actually the survivors of a cast which had been assembled at Cincinnati for the first game on October 18. The Giants won it, 11 to 2.

From that date, day by day, the tourists played their way through cities of Illinois, Iowa, Kansas, Missouri, Oklahoma, Texas, Arizona, California, and Oregon. Despite the season of the year, they were rained out but three times and Abilene, Texas; Sacramento, California; and Seattle, Washington, never did get to see the big show. When the Seattle game was rained out, and stock was taken, it was discovered that the Giants had won sixteen, the White Sox fifteen, of the thirty-one games played.

The playing membership of the party had been subjected to changes along the route, and there were some runouts as far along the line as California. Two notables who asked to be excused were Orval Overall of the Cubs and Christy Mathewson, McGraw's favorite pitcher and one of baseball's all-time greats. When these two left, McGraw was hard pressed for pitching, since George (Hooks) Wiltse and Bunny Hearn were all that remained.

Comiskey came to McGraw's relief with a suggestion which the Giant boss accepted as a stopgap. Property of the White Sox, just acquired from the Des Moines club in the Western League, was Urban (Red) Faber, who had yet to face a major-league batsman. His record of having won more than twenty games in each of the 1912 and 1913 seasons had attracted him to the White Sox.

"Why not take him along?" asked Comiskey, and McGraw assented, sight unseen. It might as well be mentioned here and now, that after watching Red pitch a few games, McGraw offered Comiskey $50,000 for him.

"If he impresses you that much," said Comiskey, "I guess he's the pitcher we've been needing in the American League. I wouldn't sell him now for five times that amount."

So Red Faber's debut with major-league ball players was against the White Sox rather than for them, though before his course was run he was to do enough pitching to more than justify Comiskey's estimate of his worth.

The two squads which sailed from Vancouver had a smattering of White Sox and Giants, but no more. Under McGraw's direction and wearing Giant uniforms were catcher Ivy Wingo, Cardinals; third baseman Hans Lobert, Phillies; shortstop Mike Doolan, Phillies; and outfielder Lee Magee, Cardinals; as well as Faber, borrowed from Comiskey's reserve list. Regulation Giants were pitchers Wiltse and Hearn, first baseman Fred Merkle, second baseman Larry Doyle, and outfielders Mike Donlin and Jim Thorpe.

With the exception of Faber, the Giants' round-the-world roster stuck to the National League. The White Sox group was not so clannish.

Manager Callahan had at his command catcher Jack Bliss, St. Louis Cardinals; third baseman Dick Egan, Cincinnati and Brooklyn; and outfielder Steve Evans, Cardinals, all National Leaguers. American League clubs other than the White Sox contributed outfielder Tris Speaker, Boston; outfielder Sam Crawford, Detroit; infielder Germany Schaefer, Washington; and pitcher Walter Leverenz, St. Louis.

The White Sox club itself furnished pitchers Jim Scott and Joe Benz; catcher Tom Daly, and shortstop Buck Weaver. But it was as White Sox and Giants they made their way around the world.

The first games on foreign soil were played at Tokyo, where enthusiastic crowds greeted the players. Baseball was in a thriving state in Japan and had been for several years, particularly as a college sport. Keio University's team had made a tour of the United States two years before. The White Sox won a pair of games from the Giants at Tokyo, and then combined to whack Keio, 16 to 3.

The umpires on this tour were Bill Klem and Jack Sheridan and it was Klem's duty to introduce each of the players as he came to bat. Most wildly acclaimed of all the tourists was Jim Thorpe, the Carlisle, Pennsylvania, outfielder of the Giants. Memory of his great feats as an Olympic athlete a few years before was fresh in the minds of all, even as far off as Japan.

One of Comiskey's friends in the noncombatant group of tourists remarked the acclaim the Japanese gave Thorpe.

"Why not," said Comiskey. "He's the only real American in the party, isn't he?"

The tour went from Japan to China, where a game was played at Hong Kong. Next stop was Manila for two games, and then a longer hop to Australia, where the cities of Brisbane, Sydney, and Melbourne were visited.

At Sydney, and again at Melbourne, the tourists deviated

from their White Sox vs. Giants program. The White Sox took on an Australian group at Sydney and beat them, 10 to 1. At Melbourne the challenge of a Victoria group was turned back by the Giants, 18 to 0.

It was in Australia that the tourists were first able to go in for a collection of press clippings since leaving Vancouver. This was long before the time of Moe Berg, the storied major-league character able to read, write, and speak most of the known languages. There was no one, from Comiskey and McGraw through both squads and the entire party of rooters, including the two correspondents, Gus Axelson of the *Chicago Record* and Joe Farrell of the *Chicago Tribune,* who was able to tell whether Japanese or Chinese sports experts liked them, or not. In Manila, what with a round of social functions, no one had time to read the daily press.

In Australia, where the party was entertained royally by Reginald (Snowy) Baker and Hugh McIntosh, the famous sportsmen, there was plenty written of the players and the play. At Sydney, where Buck Weaver's ninth-inning hit past third base scored Steve Evans and Jack Bliss and gave the White Sox a 5 to 4 victory over the Giants, an Australian journalist composed these lines:

The teams were evenly matched. Notwithstanding, there was nothing thrillingly spectacular, principally because each combination was mechanically so highly efficient and executed plays as if they could not help it. Still, many attractive features were introduced that served to keep the onlookers continuously interested.

There was plenty of hitting, smashing drives, lofty slogging, line hits, bunts, and infield smashes, all of which were cleverly handled wherever possible. The control of the pitchers, the pace of the base runners, the speed and accuracy of the throwing, the vigour and impetus of the foot-sliding, and the wonderful work of the outfielders, all contributed to a brilliant exposition of baseball.

Cynics may deride the remarkable performance of the outfielders because of the glove they use, compared with the bare hand of the cricketer; but the essence of their proficiency lies in their judgment in anticipating the flight of the ball from the bat, in gauging the distance of the hit, and in getting into position to receive the falling ball when they are not forced to rush for a running catch. The three catches by Magee, Thorpe and Speaker in left, right and centre field, which retired the White Sox in their first innings, were excellent.

The Americans cannot understand us applauding their catching. That is a phase of cricket. In the United States, unless the catch borders on the miraculous, the public seldom clap. Everybody is expected to handle every ball within reach.

Towards the finish the White Sox began to overhaul their opponents. Only one to tie in the last innings, with two out, a man on second and third, two strokes called on the striker, by name Buck Weaver. Then a splendid hit along the left line and two runners dashed to the plate, making the winning run amidst frantic excitement. It was a worthy climax to an entertaining display.

Two very uncommon incidents occurred in the game. In the Giants' second session Wingo was given out for not batting in the right order, and in the sixth inning of the White Sox Speaker was declared off for deliberately interfering with a ball thrown to beat him trying to regain his base. This led to some heckling of the umpire, Mr. Sheridan, which in America might have cost the offender several dollars in the way of a fine. That was the only little incident that disturbed the harmony of the proceedings.

From Australia the tourists went on to Ceylon, where they played a ball game and were entertained by Sir Thomas Lipton.

Then came Cairo, Egypt, and at a ball game there the White Sox and Giants appeared before royalty for the first time, for Abbas Hilmi II, Khedive of Egypt, was among the spectators. There is a question whether the ball players were of as much interest to the Khedive as he was to them, for Abbas Hilmi II appeared with forty-three of his wives and one hundred retainers. Practically incognito, reporter Joe Farrell allowed.

One of Comiskey's own faithful retainers, Norris (Tip) O'Neill, was a bit irked when the White Sox reeled off a triple play in the game and the Khedive didn't seem to be impressed.

O'Neill nudged Comiskey and protested, "He didn't even notice that triple play!"

"He's got enough to do," said Comiskey. "If you had forty-three wives to watch you wouldn't notice a triple play, either."

The tourists spent several days sight-seeing in Italy. At Rome, the only Italian city where they had been scheduled, rain prevented play. During their stay at Rome the party was given an audience by the Pope.

At Naples Cavaliere F. Bertolini, chairman of the committee on arrangements, presented Comiskey and McGraw each with a bronze statuette. McGraw's was a replica of "The Gladiator" and bore the inscription: "Baseball is the brother of war, but its battles shed no blood." Comiskey's was a copy of the "Disc Thrower" and its inscription was: "Sport is the uniter of nations and a strengthener and upbuilder of man." Both inscriptions were written especially for the statuettes by Hall Caine, who was sojourning in Naples at the time.

Nice, in France, was the next stop, and here was played

the first game of the tourists on European soil. The White Sox won it, 10 to 9, which gave them a twenty-four to twenty-one lead in the series begun at Cincinnati nearly four months before. Rain interfered with all prospect for a game in Paris, and the tourists turned toward London, the last stop before home, and the scene of the most memorable game of the entire tour.

CHAPTER NINE

THE introduction of major-league baseball to England by accredited artisans took place at Chelsea Football Grounds, Stamford Bridge, February 26, 1914.

The game might have had no more bearing on the international situation than any of the others from Japan to France were it not for the fact that the day before the game it was announced that His Majesty, George V, intended to view the proceedings. That was all right with the ball players, but it caused several anxious moments for Comiskey and the rest of the tourists not due to don White Sox or Giant uniforms.

"What does one wear when the King shows up?" was asked by Tip O'Neill, Comiskey's retainer. None could answer him.

The question of proper attire was still being debated the morning of the game in quarters in the Hotel Cecil by McGraw and Joe Farrell, Comiskey having stepped out for the moment. In the midst of the discussion a representative of His Majesty arrived, introduced himself and said he brought His Majesty's compliments to Messrs. Comiskey and McGraw.

The representative looked inquiringly at McGraw and

Farrell, the latter bowing, and seeing no reason for explaining that this was McGraw but that he was Farrell, and that Comiskey had stepped out for a quick snort.

"His Majesty conveys his compliments," droned the representative, "and wishes you to know that at this afternoon's game between the New York and Chicago teams he will wear a conventional American sack suit."

He bowed and left, whereupon, after a not too dignified interval, McGraw and Farrell made haste to get where Comiskey was, tell him the pressure was off, and join him in another snort for the sake of international amity.

Farrell, quite gifted in oratory, along with other talents, needed that bracer when Comiskey presently told him that he had been chosen to sit in the Royal Box with the King, U. S. Ambassador Walter Hines Page, and the members of the royal suite, and explain the intricacies of the game to His Majesty. In his dispatch to the *Chicago Tribune*, Farrell was content to say that he had been permitted to shake the hand of His Royal Highness.

This, however, was enough to cause Ring Lardner to wax lyrical for the benefit of Farrell's old pals in Chicago:

> I wonder, will Farrell be just as of old
> And treat us as equals and chums?
> Or will he be distant and offish and cold
> And snobbish and mean to us bums?
> Will it be presumption to buy him a drink
> Since Farrell, Joe Farrell, shook hands with the
>   Kink?
>
> He used to be so democratic and nice
> The pal of us poor common folks
> O, will he now freeze us with glances of ice?
> Regard us as pests and as jokes?
> I never will feel quite at home with the gink
> Since Farrell, Joe Farrell, shook hands with the
>   Kink.

Lardner's fears were unwarranted, for Farrell didn't change a bit—hasn't yet, in fact, as he puts in his time publicizing the efforts of Chicago's ice-hockey team, the Black Hawks. But he retains vivid recollections of the day he explained baseball to the King.

"I started out," he said, "trying to be very factual about everything, and refrain from using baseball expressions that were common to us. The King seemed to be an interested listener and he asked some questions. Most of the time he just watched and said nothing.

"There came a time in the game when the score was tied at 2 to 2 and the White Sox got a runner on third base, with two out. I volunteered that this was a crucial point in the game, and explained that if the White Sox got that run in, the way Jim Scott was pitching, it might decide the ball game. I explained in detail all the ways the run might come in, such as on a hit, an error, a wild pitch, a passed ball. The man on third, I said, could even steal home, though I remarked that this was unusual.

"The King just looked at me politely, nodded now and then, and finally turned to the field. Just then the batter hit up a dinky foul that the third baseman caught, retiring the side. The King turned around to me and said: 'A most useful catch, wasn't it?' I still don't know whether he had been spoofing me, all the time."

The presence of the King at the game, the final engagement of the world tour, was hailed by Comiskey as a glorious climax.

"Kindnesses galore have been showered upon us on this trip," he said, "but today's reception was the top of all. The King's decision to attend the game came as a delightful surprise. Many eminent Englishmen had joined the Americans in London in assuring us that we were welcome, but evidence of the feeling scarcely had shown itself in some of the leading newspapers. Why, I do not know. What the people at large were thinking, I had no means of ascertaining.

"While we were on pins and needles as to our reception, King George authorized the statement that he would attend the game. The change that swept over the press was electric and our visit immediately became an event of the first importance. Those newspapers which previously had given us little attention or had spoken of us rather caustically opened their columns to news of the game.

"We appreciate profoundly the interest of the King. We came here as friends of the English people, not with intent to displace cricket, not to flaunt claims of the superiority of baseball over English games, but merely to give an exhibition of our national sport for what it was worth. The King understood and extended us the hand of good fellowship. This action is not only a beautiful instance of friendship and good manners but a fine example of statesmanlike intuition."

Nor was Comiskey less elated when Ambassador Page asserted that the game was the greatest thing Americans had ever staged in London. The "electric" change that Comiskey said swept over the London press when the King approved the baseball show saw to it that every phase of the visit was duly chronicled. London readers knew what the White Sox–Giants party ate, where they ate it, what they wore, who they saw, how they talked, and to whom. There were furnished glossaries of American baseball lingo, duly translated into Londonese. There were interviews galore, and some of them, if they ever caught the eye of a Chicago reader, might have caused the lifting of an eyebrow or two. Such as the little chat a reporter of *The Daily Mirror* had with the White Sox pitcher, Joe Benz, the "Butcher Boy":

How to throw a ball which after traveling in a straight line for some ten or fifteen yards begins suddenly to make amazing "hairpin" curves around the batsman, was described to *The Daily Mirror* yesterday by Mr. "Joe" Benz, one of America's most famous pitchers.

He has a claim to baseball fame for he invented the "spit" ball and improved the "shadow" ball.

Mr. Benz is the pitcher for the Chicago "White Sox" team who will battle with the New York "Giants" in today's exhibition game at the Chelsea Football Grounds at Stamford Bridge.

A big, powerful young man with a sunny smile, "Joe" Benz is the idol of American schoolboys and baseball "fans."

His specialty is the "spit" ball which puzzles scientists and is the daily wonder of the crowd.

"See those two fingers," he said, holding up his right hand. The first two fingers were twisted in curious fashion. "That is the result of putting the 'twist' on the ball when I pitch it to the batsman at the home base.

"Why the ball behaves as it does, I cannot explain—I simply know how to do it. By a movement of the fingers—and the ball leaves me at lightning pace—I can make it twist and turn in different directions when it reaches the base."

Benz, the Butcher Boy, turned up in the afternoon as the winning pitcher of record. He relieved Jim Scott in the sixth, and was in charge in the eleventh when Tommy Daly hit a home run that gave the White Sox the ball game, 5 to 4.

As a game of baseball, played anywhere else but in the presence of the King, the contest would have been thrilling enough. Viewed through the eyes of some 30,000 spectators, many of whom were seeing a baseball game for the first time, it was something else again.

The White Sox picked up two runs in the third inning when Red Faber's error put Steve Evans on base, and Jack Bliss reached first when Fred Merkle forgot to cover the base. (The same Merkle, against another Chicago team, six years before, had forgotten to touch second base, and thereby took his place in baseball history. But his oversight here went right by the Stamford Bridge crowd, save for the sprinkling of Americans present who remembered the mighty ruckus created by the Cubs' Johnny Evers when Merkle pulled his historic 1908 boner that cost the Giants a pennant.)

Buck Weaver drove both Evans and Bliss home, to put the White Sox in the lead, but Hans Lobert's homer scoring Lee Magee ahead of him in the fourth evened the count. In the tenth inning the Giants clustered hits by Mike Donlin, Magee, and Lobert, and these with a pair of infield outs brought in two runs.

Just when it looked as if the ball game were over, Weaver came through with a single in the White Sox half, and Sam Crawford promptly hit for the circuit. Once again the score was tied. Benz got by the Giants neatly in their half of the eleventh, and then came Daly's clout, the longest hit of the ball game. This home run, third of the day, gave the White Sox their 5 to 4 victory.

CHAPTER TEN

No chronicle of the appearance of the White Sox and Giants before the King would be complete if it did not include London newspaper accounts of the gala day.

From a variety of stories, the following have been selected, and before absorbing them the reader is cautioned to brush up on the details of the game with which the previous chapter ended. Said one report of the game itself:

> The King was present at the Chelsea Football Grounds, Stamford Bridge, yesterday afternoon to witness the baseball match between the two American teams, the New York Giants and Chicago White Sox. His Majesty was received by the American Ambassador, who sat with him and explained the points of the game, the King asking many questions. His Majesty remained until the end of the match, which resulted in a win for Chicago by five runs to four.
>
> The game was watched by about 30,000 spectators, and considering the stickiness of the ground, the play was of a very high order. At the end of the nine innings the score stood 2—2. The 10th innings was extremely dramatic and produced two runs to each side, making

William "Kid" Gleason, manager of the 1919 "Black Sox," with Clarence Rowland, manager of the world champion 1917 Sox. (*The Sporting News.*)

George "Buck" Weaver, third base. (The Sporting News.)

Charles "Swede" Risberg, shortstop. (The Sporting News.)

Eddie Cicotte, pitcher. (The Sporting News.)

Members of the 1919 Chicago White Sox

the score 4—4. New York failed to score in the 11th, and Daly, the first man to go to bat for Chicago, hit a magnificent home run and won the match.

Perhaps the greatest incident of the match was in Chicago's 10th innings. The score was 4—2 in favour of New York, and Chicago had two men out, with one (Weaver) on second base when Crawford came to bat. The situation cried aloud for a home run—and it came, the batsman lifting the ball gorgeously over the head of the left field into the middle of the spectators in the further stand scoring (Weaver being on second base) the two runs necessary to tie the match. It was hard on Faber who pitched finely throughout the game; but it was superb.

There were, however, many thrilling incidents. In Chicago's eighth innings an extraordinarily brilliant piece of work by Merkle put Bliss out by a matter of inches at the home plate as he came in from third base, and for the moment saved the game for the Giants. Magee's performance at left field again and again roused the spectators to enthusiasm. One catch in particular, when he took a flyer from Daly with his left hand high up against the rails, was almost too spectacular to be "good ball." On the other hand it was bad fumbling in the short field that allowed Chicago in the third innings to get three men on bases before one was out, so that when Weaver got the ball away cleanly to the boundary, Evans and Bliss came home and gave Chicago the first two runs of the match. It was poor fielding again which enabled Magee in New York's next innings to get to first base, so that when Lobert hit a great home run the score was equalized. Such things, however, were very few and the bad condition of the ground more than excused them. In compensation there were some brilliant double plays, notably in Chicago's fourth innings, in which Lobert, Doyle and Merkle took part. Faber pitched very well throughout for New York. For Chicago Scott, who is reputed the best pitcher in either team, grew a trifle wild in the fifth innings and was succeeded by Benz, who did extremely well in the trying final periods. The catching (in the American sense) of Wingo, Bliss and Slight was faultless.

English spectators, to whom the game was new, must yesterday have received certain definite impressions. First, it is clearly "glorified rounders." Of course it has been immensely developed, and the fielders no longer have the youthful joy of "corking" the ball as hard as possible at the fleeing batsman. It is superbly organized and specialized in every detail; but the framework of the old English village game still remains. Secondly, in batting, in spite of all the gorgeous smiting that was seen, baseball does not compare with cricket. Next, the cleverness and the velocity of the pitching are wonderful.

Finally, there is no fielding in cricket which approaches the fielding and throwing which were seen yesterday.

The catching (in the cricket sense) was extremely good; but the real marvel of the game was the almost indescribable suddenness and accuracy of the returns. It is little exaggeration to say that in the double plays (when two batsmen are put off the same stroke) the eye had difficulty in following the movements and flight of the ball. The throwing from all points was approximately perfect. The catching (again in the cricket sense) almost as perfect, and in the case of both Merkle and Daly, at 1st base, quite beyond praise.

Before the game began (the King did not arrive until a few minutes before 3 o'clock) an exhibition of hitting, fielding and throwing was given by members of the two teams, which delighted the spectators, one excellent piece of fooling being when the New York men for several minutes played with an imaginary ball.

Members of the crowd contributed their share to the entertainment by pleading with the pitcher to kill the batsmen, and the way the umpire called the strikes and balls and delivered his decisions was a joy. Altogether it was an excellent game but, to English spectators— it was not cricket. It cannot be said that the crowd showed any evidence of thinking that baseball is ever likely to supersede our national game.

The rival teams were as follows:

GIANTS (White Jerseys)		WHITE SOX (Blue Jerseys)
Donlin	center field	Speaker
Magee	left field	Evans
Lobert	third base	Egan
Doyle	second base	Schaefer
Merkle	first base	Daly
Doolan	shortstop	Weaver
Thorpe	right field	Crawford
Wingo	catcher	Bliss
Faber	pitcher	Scott

UMPIRE—Mr. Will Klem

The London baseball writer (pro tem) is to be pardoned for confusing a baseball batting order with a football line-up. The Giants actually batted as listed above, but the White Sox went to bat in this wise: Weaver ss; Egan 3b; Speaker cf; Crawford rf; Schaefer 2b; Daly 1b; Evans lf; Bliss c; Scott and Benz p.

One other bit of factual reporting, which seemed to hit the fancy of Messrs. Farrell and Axelson, Chicago trained— at the end of the game the Earl of Chesterfield reported to the police that he had been robbed of a scarfpin valued at five hundred pounds.

Now for some further reaction of the English writers to the first visitation of skilled practitioners of America's national pastime.

First, the analyst, who wrote in part as follows:

53

The game is, of course, rounders sophisticated, not glorified, because the glory of rounders, the right of the fielder to "cork" the opponent running from base to base, is removed by law from baseball. The sophistication consists mainly in the marking out of the playing area. The batsman stands at the apex of a right-angled triangle, and any of his hits which pitches behind the sides of the triangle is a "foul"; if he makes four such fouls before hitting a ball within bounds he is out; but if he can carry the hypotenuse of the triangle he scores a complete run for his side. In passing it may be said that the Stamford Bridge ground is of a size which made his carry too easy. Thrice yesterday the ball pitched among the people on the far side, a fact which offended the pundits in the Grand Stand.

The effect of circumscribing the playing area on either side of the batter, combined with the character of the implements used, gives an overwhelming advantage to the fielders. The bat is a round club, some three inches in diameter at its thickest part; the ball is practically of the same size and weight as a cricket ball, but softer and easier to catch; it is also covered with a charmingly sympathetic leather, which invites the fingers to grip it closely for the purpose of making it spin.

The pitcher is allowed to throw as hard as he pleases from a distance of twenty yards, and as he has learned to impart all manner of cunning swerves to his missile, it is obvious that the keenest sighted of batters can only make a clean stroke by the merest chance. This is the more true because the batter is necessarily limited to strokes of two kinds. He can attempt to full shouldered "cow shot" or, in the terminology of the game, "bunt" the ball a short distance with a cross bat push from the elbows. Yesterday the cow shot came off about a half a dozen times and then the ball flew a tidy long way. More often the result was a skier on the roof of the stand behind the striker. Not all the magnificence of the catching and stopping by all the fielders, nor all the unfailing accuracy and power of their throwing, could compensate for the dullness of repeated failure with the bat.

Few of the spectators were sufficiently well educated to appreciate the cleverness of the teams in their tactical moves, but the general principles of the game were easy to pick up. The pitcher aimed to throw the ball over a white plate, which looked some two feet wide. The batter, standing by this plate, tries to hit away so that he can at least reach first base distant thirty yards to his right front, before the fielder can return the ball to his colleague posted to guard that position. If the pitcher is four times wide of the plate the batter is allowed to proceed to first base without more ado. But if the batter fails three times to strike a straight ball he is out. He is also out if a hit of his is caught. Any player who succeeds in making good his ground at each of the three bases and at the home plate, scores a run, and it is not necessary for him to complete the circuit off a hit of his own. The innings of a side terminates when three of its men are put out.

Baseball may be an exciting game to play; it certainly provides openings for combined work in the field, and the "kidding" tricks of a crafty poker player are obviously of value. But it offers a very poor spectacle compared with cricket and football. One cannot see what the pitcher is doing; his swerves have to be taken on trust. And the very patent disabilities of the batter, as has been said, destroy that balance of attack and defense which is essential to the interest of an athletic contest. It cannot take on in England until we have forgotten what it has taken us centuries to learn, that the fun of a ball game consists mainly in hitting the ball.

Too bad the London analyst of 1914 didn't get to see our national game since the lively ball was introduced, and the home run became a "must" for crowd appeal.

Now for an editorial writer:

America's national game came and showed itself to England at Chelsea yesterday, and the King—"no mean judge of sports in any of its branches," as Lord Desborough has well described him—was there to watch an exciting match. Baseball is the game of a hundred millions of people, and it is, on the other side of the Atlantic, as much a ceremony and an obsession as cricket is on this side. We do not think baseball will ever oust cricket from this country, or that it can be transplanted with success, and we need not regret the fact. Each man and nation to an individual choice, and we do well to cling to cricket, America to baseball. Only those who play a game understand and appreciate it. No one but the Eton Colleger really knows and loves the bewildering wall game. Only the pitcher or catcher or fielder understands baseball truly. And for games, as for good government, sympathy is the secret of success. But this baseball match has shown us much to admire and to emulate—much very brilliant fielding which may well stir the cricketer to admiration and even envy. It has shown us keenness in the individual and keenness for the side that are the best elements of true sport. It has shown us other English speaking sportsmen playing the game as it should be played. We may stick to our cricket. But we shall not make the mistake of despising baseball.

To complete this cross section of England's outlook on America's national pastime—first glimpse of which was afforded in 1889 when A. G. Spalding's tourists visited London—there was a letter to the editor of the *Daily Chronicle:*

Sir—On March 12, 1889, a game at baseball by American players was played at Kensington Oval. The then

56

Prince of Wales (Edward VII) was present. The *New York Herald* invited criticism of the game on cards distributed for the purpose, and I now have a copy of the next day's paper before me. The Prince of Wales said: "The Prince of Wales has witnessed the game of baseball with great interest, and though he considers it an excellent game, he considers cricket as superior."

A. MILLARD

Sidcup, Feb. 26.

CHAPTER ELEVEN

In plotting the course of Comiskey and his White Sox, it may seem that Byron Bancroft Johnson, or "BB" as Comiskey called him, has departed from this story of a team and a league. He has not. Indeed, the relationship between Comiskey and Johnson was an endless succession of clashes of temperament, as each grew in baseball importance. Deep down, they were friends, as they had been from their early days in Cincinnati, and wanted to remain such to the end, but Fate decreed otherwise.

In their leisure moments both were royal hosts, and if Johnson established more of a reputation as a quick-tempered roisterer, it can hardly be said that Comiskey or Comiskey's cronies, who were many, did not create more than one situation which was fanned into a friendship-consuming flame. At his new ball park Comiskey established a gathering place for his friends, who, because of frequent excursions into Wisconsin to relax as Comiskey's guests at a hunting lodge, were known as the Woodland Bards. They were a drinking crowd for the most part, and practical jokers, one and all.

On one of the Wisconsin excursions, Johnson took along with him a new shotgun and a fine suède hunting jacket with racks for shells. Ban was very proud of both, and considerable fuss was made over them by members of the party.

The trail to the camp involved an overnight ride in a train, an early morning arrival, and an all-day jaunt by buckboard to the ultimate destination. It was common practice for the Nimrods to blaze away at partridge along the buckboard route.

Johnson could hardly wait to get the preferred seat at the front of the buckboard to try out his new gun, but he was persuaded, upon alighting from the train, to enter a hotel dining room for breakfast—and other fortification. To be more comfortable, he put the precious gun out in the hallway and hung up the hunting vest. While he was at breakfast, one of the Bards replaced the lead pellets in all the shells with wads, and sat back to await developments. They were not long in coming.

The buckboard had traveled but a short distance when Johnson spied a partridge close up and blazed away. Nothing happened. A bit later Johnson fired at another bird, with no more success. By now he was fretting over the new gun. Its stock must be misshapen, or shortened.

"You're just a rotten shot, so don't alibi," said Comiskey, and Johnson flared up.

When camp was reached in the evening, Johnson took the gun apart and examined it closely. He worked on it for hours, and early next morning he was out for another test. Partridge abounded in that country, but none of it was as much as nicked by Johnson's shooting. Even a sitting bird, at which he fired almost from point-blank range, did no more than look annoyed at being disturbed by all the noise. In desperation Johnson finally pinned a piece of paper to a tree, advanced within a few feet of it, and fired away. Then the realization came to him of the joke that had been played upon him. His rage knew no bounds, and he blamed the whole matter on Comiskey.

"I didn't think Commy would do that to me," he said, and it was a long time after that before he would even speak to the White Sox owner. Comiskey felt keenly this break with his old friend, but did not go out of his way to make amends.

In the midst of the 1913 season, while the Sox were well up in the race, Johnson took off for Wisconsin on a fishing trip.

The White Sox were then alternating Jimmy Callahan and Ducky Holmes in left field, and Callahan was given permission to make a trip to Massachusetts. On the day of Johnson's return from the fishing trip, Holmes became involved in a dispute with an umpire and was bounced out of the game.

The following morning when Comiskey reached his office at the park, a fine string of bass awaited him, a present from Johnson. Comiskey beamed at this, and literally had the string of fish on exhibition, as each of his friends dropped in the Bards Room. "Look what 'BB' sent me," Comiskey kept repeating, and his friends rejoiced with him that this was a token that the enmity of the President for Comiskey had come to an end.

Comiskey had the string of fish on display for a new set of arrivals when a messenger from the American League office arrived with a notice for Comiskey that Johnson, having studied his umpire's report, was hereby suspending outfielder Holmes indefinitely.

"What does that fat So and So expect *me* to do?" raged Comiskey, "Play this string of bass in left field?"

And with a sweep of his arm he pitched the bass into Thirty-fifth Street, and the breach between him and Johnson was wider than ever.

Another attempt to patch it up was made in the spring

of 1914 when Johnson was persuaded to make a trip on the White Sox special train to California, when the club left for spring training. These special trains were introduced by Comiskey in 1908 and were an annual adventure for the "Old Roman" and his host of fun-loving followers.

Tip O'Neill, one of Comiskey's closest cronies, and an anti-Johnson man, was usually the life of the party on these trips. His exact place in the Comiskey ménage was never quite clear. Perhaps an odd-job man might have been his proper description. He was unquestionably faithful, according to his lights. He was an expert on California affairs, or so he claimed, and often served as advance man for White Sox spring exhibition tours in that state.

One spring he was approached by Dutch Leonard, the Boston Red Sox pitcher, a resident of Fresno. Leonard represented a team he had organized in his home town. Most California towns and smaller cities maintained independent teams in those days, play usually being restricted to Sunday games. Generally the personnel was of the semipro sort, but in the off season, players from the major leagues and various minor leagues frequently joined up, for a carrying charge.

O'Neill knew Fresno was not too large a city. When Leonard suggested a modest guarantee instead of a percentage of the gate receipts, O'Neill accepted the guarantee before Leonard had a chance to change his mind.

The day the game was played fans from all parts of that raisin-growing area poured into the ball park. The percentage the White Sox might have had would have topped the modest guarantee that O'Neill accepted, many times over. For a long time thereafter Comiskey kidded O'Neill about this, once saying that he wondered if it might not be wiser to have someone who didn't know California arrange the White Sox exhibition schedule.

On this particular 1914 trip, O'Neill's constant needling

of Comiskey on the subject of Johnson precipitated several awkward moments. The climax came at a party in San Francisco, when Comiskey was finally moved to let Johnson have it, chapter and verse. He recited all his grievances against the league president from 1900 on. He wound up extending his guest the freedom of the great outdoors.

Diplomatic relations between the two were now broken off for the last time. Their mutual feeling from then on was one of dislike, but it took a subsequent adverse ruling of Johnson on a strictly baseball matter to turn this dislike into positive hatred. The break between Johnson and Comiskey was eventually to threaten the whole structure of the American League. It actually did lead to a complete reorganization of baseball's administrative system.

On their return from California on this eventful spring trip, the White Sox plunged into the pennant race, which was to mark Callahan's last appearance as their manager. It also focused attention on two of the pitchers who had been on the trip around the world. Each turned in a game which will stand among the freak pitching accomplishments.

On May 14, pitching against Washington, Jim Scott negotiated a no-hit, no-run game for nine innings—and lost in the tenth, 1 to 0.

Seventeen days later, against Cleveland, Joe Benz, who the English writer thought had invented the spitball, delivered a no hitter, and won, 6 to 1.

At the end of the season, with his club anchored in sixth place, Comiskey was more determined than ever, because of the break with Johnson, to assemble a team of championship status as quickly as possible. To do this he hit upon the idea of a complete change of tactics in choice of manager, and of fields in which to search for the kind of playing talent Comiskey Park needed and which Comiskey Park must have.

The 1915 season was the dawn of a new era for the White Sox. It introduced a cast of characters, one of whom at least will always be remembered around Comiskey Park and by all White Sox friends and followers, whatever their persuasion.

This new force in White Sox affairs was Harry Grabiner, who as a small boy had come to Comiskey's attention in 1905. One morning the boss of the White Sox was doing the best he could with a limited staff trying to get a rain-soaked field in shape that it might be played upon in the afternoon, when in wandered the small boy, Grabiner, and asked if there was anything he could do to help.

There was, then. There was, thereafter. Anything and everything around Comiskey Park, until the time came when Comiskey leaned on Grabiner more than on any of his other friends, associates, or employees. By the end of the 1915 season, the young man-about-Comiskey-Park, Grabiner, had accepted a portfolio as secretary of the club.

He was to go on, and on, from there.

CHAPTER TWELVE

IN the first fourteen years of their existence, the White Sox had experienced a steady turnover of managers. Comiskey, the original leader, turned the job over to Clark Griffith. After Griffith's term, Jimmy Callahan, Fielder Jones, Billy Sullivan, Hugh Duffy, and Callahan for a return engagement took their turns. All but Duffy had been players who served under Comiskey, and the veteran Duffy was a contemporary of Comiskey toward the end of the latter's playing career.

With all of his managers, Comiskey found the same fault. He liked to be consulted about the plays and the players, but his managers, one after another, were not going into executive session with him often enough. Moreover, when Comiskey made suggestions out of his own vast store of baseball knowledge, they were not always followed out.

For the 1915 season then, he resolved on a radical change in field leaders. He went completely out of the major-league ranks, past and current, to get his next manager. His choice was Clarence Rowland, whose playing career had been restricted to some minor-league catching. However, he came to the White Sox after having done a capable job of managing at Peoria in the 1914 season.

Rowland was not only amenable to advice from the "Old Roman" but openly courted it, and he and Comiskey hit it off from scratch.

Given a manager with no major-league experience, Comiskey then decided that the proper thing to do was to outfit him with some players of proven skill in the American League.

Though the ill feeling between Comiskey and Ban Johnson was still in existence, the league president recognized the value to the organization of having a successful team in Chicago. Word had reached Johnson through channels that Connie Mack, following the 1914 slaughter of his supposed invincible Philadelphia Athletics by the Boston Braves, was preparing to break up his team. He passed the tip along to Comiskey, and the White Sox owner went into the market.

Johnson was also looking after the interests of other clubs in the league, notably the Boston Red Sox. But when it came time to negotiate for the services of Eddie Collins, Connie Mack's asking price was such that only Comiskey was interested—which was exactly as Johnson had hoped.

Collins was the key man in what had been termed the "$100,000 infield." Frank (Home Run) Baker, Jack Barry, and Stuffy McInnis were the others. Mack's asking price of $50,000 for Collins was a new high for baseball material, but Comiskey did not back away from it. Getting the $50,000 to Mack was just part of the problem, for Collins, no mean hand at estimating his own value, had to be satisfied as well.

He demanded a five year contract at $15,000 a season, which straightway placed him among the highest-salaried players of the time. Moreover, he wanted a $15,000 bonus for signing, though some still say that was Johnson's idea, rather than Collins'. He got the bonus, and the White Sox were assured one half of an infield that was to make baseball history, for Buck Weaver, whether at short or at third, had already captured the fancy of Comiskey and the White Sox fans.

The baseball grapevine next brought the news to Comiskey that there was a possibility Cleveland, for a price, might relinquish the services of outfielder Joe Jackson, then recognized as one of the great batsmen of all time.

Jackson, an uneducated and uncouth man, was known as "Shoeless Joe," the appellation being traced back to his earlier days in the Carolinas where he was required to play on a field that was rough and strewn with boulders, broken bottles, and other impedimenta. After coursing around the uneven terrain in his bare feet for a few innings, Jackson announced that he wasn't going to play on such a rough field any longer.

"If it's too rough for your feet, why don't you put on shoes?" Jackson was asked.

"Who said anything about my feet?" snapped Jackson. "My feet ain't bothering me. It's the ball. It's getting so wingy from that rough cow pasture I can't throw it."

They had succeeded in putting shoes on Jackson long before he joined Cleveland to become a batting genius.

Having heard that there was an outside chance to land this player, Comiskey called his secretary, Harry Grabiner, and handed him a signed blank check.

"I want Jackson," said Comiskey. "Don't come back without him."

That was all the instruction Grabiner needed.

He moved on president Charles W. Somers of the Cleveland club, waving the blank check gently to and fro.

Sure, Jackson was for sale. Anybody was for sale, providing the price was right.

"Shoeless" Joe Jackson, left fielder. (*The Sporting News.*)

Arnold "Chick" Gandil, first baseman. (*The Sporting News.*)

Oscar "Happy" Felsch, center fielder. (*The Sporting News.*)

Claude Williams, pitcher. (*The Sporting News.*)

Members of the 1919 Chicago White Sox

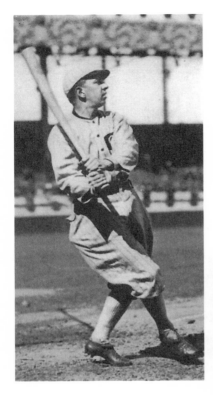

Eddie Collins, the White Sox great second baseman and manager for the 1925 and 1926 seasons. (*The Sporting News.*)

Ray Schalk, one of the game's great catchers; player, and in 1927-1928, manager for the White Sox. (*The Sporting News.*)

"How much?" asked Grabiner.

The deal was closed for $31,500 cash, and the option to take three players from the White Sox reserve list. The players were Larry Chappell, who had cost $18,000; Bobby Roth, who had cost $11,000, and Ed Klepfer, who had cost $5,000.

The sum of $31,500 in cash and $34,000 in players—$65,500 in all—was what Grabiner's jaunt to Cleveland had cost Comiskey. The young secretary was a bit fearful to return to Comiskey Park and face his boss after this record outlay for a single player.

He needn't have been. When he entered the Comiskey presence, he was commended by the "Old Roman." "If only everyone in my employ would do what I ask them to," sighed Comiskey.

Now the White Sox possessed the makings of a great infield, and in Jackson they had a superlative batsman and a passable defensive player. They already had, in Ray Schalk, one of the game's great catchers.

Milwaukee, whence Schalk had come a few years before, had in "Happy" Felsch an outfielder of great promise. He could be obtained for $12,000. He was. He lasted to take his place with Bill Lange, Tris Speaker, and in baseball's later stages, Joe DiMaggio, as the greatest of center fielders.

The pitching staff was beginning to take shape, and Comiskey's championship experience, dating back to 1906, had taught him no title was to be expected until he had a set of hurlers capable of starting and then finishing what they started.

Red Faber, whose adventures in the 'round-the-world tour had brought him more attention from Comiskey than might otherwise have been the case, had an average year through 1914 when he won ten and lost nine. The 1915 season saw him take his place with the league's best, for he won twenty-four games while losing thirteen.

Joe Benz and Jim Scott lingered on, though neither was to have too profound effect on the White Sox future.

In from Boston drifted the veteran, Eddie Cicotte, who had been working the American League pitching beat since joining Detroit in 1905. He was an accomplished artist who specialized in a pitch peculiarly his own, known as the "shine ball." He had not figured too greatly in Boston's plans at any time. It is improbable that Bill Carrigan, the Red Sox manager, ever regretted letting him go to the White Sox, since in the 1915 and 1916 seasons the Red Sox were masters of all they surveyed and ruled as world's champions, conquering first the Phillies and next the Dodgers.

The White Sox, though coming right along, were unable to match the craftsmanship of Carrigan's club in either of these two seasons, but they were gaining. They finished second in 1916, as against third in 1915 when Rowland and the new policy of spending money to make money and win games at the same time was inaugurated by the "Old Roman."

As proof that their loyal fans were coming out of the taprooms to pay to see the White Sox play rather than prove their devotion by heated argument outside the park, a study of the attendance figures for the 1916 season showed a lift to 679,923. This was the largest seasonal attendance in the sixteen years of White Sox history. Its increase of 140,462 from the 1915 mark was an indication that the fans were willing to go along with the new deal. They had been skeptical at first of the untried and comparatively unknown manager. Rowland was following a succession of player-managers, all of them heroic figures, and was decidedly on the spot.

Comiskey himself was championship minded. A winner, and nothing else, was what he craved. Indeed, a winner became such an obsession with him that a story was told of his entertaining a party of his friends at a Chicago restaurant featuring broiled lobster. When his own was served he noticed that a claw had been partly broken off. Comiskey sent for the head waiter and called his attention to the maimed lobster. The head waiter was ready with an explanation. Didn't Mr. Comiskey know that lobsters in their native habitat often engaged in fights, and that it was not unusual for one to have a broken claw.

"This one was in a fight, and finished like that?" inquired the "Old Roman," very quietly.

"Yes, Mr. Comiskey," nodded the waiter.

"Then," roared Comiskey, "take the damn thing away and bring *me* the winner!"

CHAPTER THIRTEEN

COMISKEY had his winner in 1917, while the world he had so recently toured with John McGraw was plunged into war.

In this year Rowland, in his third season, steered the White Sox to one hundred victories. He saw two of his pitchers, Eddie Cicotte, the veteran, and Red Faber, the youngster, come through with earned run averages of 1.53 and 1.93 respectively. This was indication that the White Sox pitching in the world's series would be in good hands.

By coincidence, the White Sox opponents in their first world's series since 1908 were McGraw's Giants, their traveling companions on the world tour. Still attached to the White Sox were Buck Weaver, Joe Benz, and Jim Scott of those who had followed Comiskey around the world. But gone from McGraw's roster were all of those who had worn Giant regalia on the playing fields of Japan, Australia, India, France, and England. McGraw alone remained. Faber, who had pitched as a "Giant" on the tour, on loan from Comiskey, was now back where he belonged. Very much so.

They were a rough and ready lot, these White Sox and Giants of 1917. They were masters of cutting repartee and they were always willing to fight for every point. Or were before the series began.

At a clubhouse meeting of the White Sox it was decided that the proper policy would be to ignore the Giants' taunts, and pretend they weren't even in the park. Word had come to them that McGraw, the scrappiest of all the managers of his time, had ordered an all out offensive. His Giants had blown three world's series in the past half-dozen years, and McGraw didn't like that, one bit.

There was one exception McGraw made in his outlining targets for abuse. That was Buck Weaver, the White Sox shortstop. On the trip around the world McGraw had seen enough of Weaver to know the sort of character he was. "Let him alone," cautioned the Giants' manager. "Don't stir him up. If you do, he'll ruin you."

Play in the series began at Comiskey Park, with 32,000 fans present.

The opening game pitted Cicotte against Slim Sallee, a Giant left-hander, and went to the White Sox, 2 to 1. A home run by Happy Felsch was the deciding factor. Otherwise the game was routine.

The second engagement, also at Comiskey Park, brought Red Faber into action for the first time. His original opponent was Ferdie Schupp, but this day the White Sox had their batting togs on and before the game ended they had manhandled Schupp, Fred Anderson, Poll Perritt, and Jeff Tesreau, winning in a canter, 7 to 2. Fourteen hits were gathered from the delivery of the Giant hurlers, Weaver and Joe Jackson setting the pace with three each.

Following an unsteady second inning in which the Giants scored both of their runs—the White Sox promptly squaring the count as soon as they could get to bat—Faber went steadily on to the first of the three victories that were to be his in the series. Contrary to expectations, however it was not Faber's magnificent pitching which sent the fans away from Comiskey Park talking to themselves about him, but his spectacular attempt to establish his prowess as a base runner.

He had made a hit in the fifth inning—every member of the line-up except right fielder John Collins shared in the fourteen-hit rout of the Giants—and eventually got to second base. Buck Weaver was at third, and two were out. Then it was that ambition to emulate Ty Cobb hit Faber. As Perritt wound up, Red lit out for third. He made it with something to spare, at the end of a marvelous head-first slide. He looked up and found his old pal, Weaver, already in possession of the base and glaring down at him.

"Where in hell do you think you're going?" Weaver wanted to know.

"Back to pitch," grinned Faber, ruefully.

When the White Sox reached New York for the continuation of the series, they were confident that their policy of ignoring the Giants' taunts was the proper one. But in the three days that elapsed between the second and third game because of adverse weather, something happened to the program.

In the familiar setting of the Polo Grounds, McGraw's club had a way with them. The crowd of 33,616 were practically all rabid Giant fans.

Rube Benton came out for his first showing of the series, and only Eddie Collins and Weaver caused him much trouble. His five-hit ball game, Weaver and Collins getting two each and Happy Felsch the other, kept the White Sox scoreless. Cicotte, winner of the opening game, was back for another try. Though he allowed but two runs—Davy Robertson with three hits being his principal annoyance—the shine-ball exponent was defeated, 2 to 0.

Another shutout was pinned on the White Sox the next day when the Giants squared the series, winning 5 to 0, on Ferdie Schupp's seven hitter. Manager Rowland, who was committed to a policy of starting Faber when he didn't start Cicotte, had come back with Red. This time Faber ran into a couple of Polo Grounds home runs by Benny Kauff, along with eight hits of assorted sizes and shapes by the rest of the cast. After the first Giant break-through in the third inning, the White Sox were never really in the ball game.

On the way back to Chicago the White Sox decided that the situation called for a change in tactics. From now on the muffler was to be taken off. They would fly at the Giants as soon as they appeared at Comiskey Park. When the Giants came on the field for the fifth game they proceeded to indulge in loosening up throwing exercises in front of their dugout. The White Sox were at batting practice. Weaver was taking his swings, when the Giants were startled by a vocal volley that topped even their own choice assortment of free-style language.

Nor was that all. By prearrangement, Weaver had the batting practice pitcher ease up and direct his pitches to the outside of the plate. Then pitch after pitch, Weaver deliberately deflected, scattering line drive fouls through the assembled Giants and causing consternation in their ranks. While some of them fled to safety, others stood their ground, being Giants, and wanted to know what was coming off.

"I'm serving notice," yelled Weaver. "From here in we're going to be tough."

From there in, tough they were, indeed, though it took them seven innings to make the Giants really believe it.

Rowland abandoned his Cicotte or Faber pitching program to start Reb Russell in this fifth game. Russell had been able to win fifteen games during the season, but had not retired a man in his first world's series inning when Cicotte came to his rescue. He held sway until the end of the sixth when Swede Risberg batted for him. Lefty

Williams then worked an inning. He went out for another pinch hitter, Byrd Lynn, in the seventh when the White Sox finally caught up with Slim Sallee and batted across three runs to tie the score at 5 to 5. Faber, nobody else, took up the pitching in the eighth and held the Giants hitless.

In their half of the inning the White Sox drove out Sallee, scoring three runs, which were more than they needed for their 8 to 5 victory, since Faber pitched a hitless ninth inning and was credited with his second win in the series.

In this game, more than any other in the series, the hitters were greatly in evidence. The White Sox made fourteen hits in all. Collins, Jackson, and Felsch collected three each. Davy Robertson, Giant right fielder who was to top all the series batsmen with eleven for twenty-two and a .500 average, came out of this free-swinging party with three more for his collection.

All this left the White Sox one up, and one to go. They made it two days later, at New York. Faber was sufficiently rested, because of the delay, to scatter six hits among the Giants and win, 4 to 2, to take his place among the rare set of pitchers who have won three games in one world's series.

The downfall of the Giants in this final game was more the result of a breakdown of their confidence by the White Sox pressure than anything else. Three of the White Sox four runs were scored in the third inning when third baseman Heinie Zimmerman executed a two-base wild throw on a chance from Eddie Collins, and Davy Robertson followed this bad break for the Giants by dropping a simple fly propelled his way by Joe Jackson.

But Zimmerman was just warming up. Shortly after this lapse, Heinie found himself in the uncomfortable spot of having the baseball at third base, with Collins between

74

him and the home plate, and streaking for the pay-off station.

Bill Rariden, the normal guardian of the plate, was A.W.O.L. Walter Holke, the first baseman, who might have covered, didn't think about it in time. Rube Benton, the pitcher, merely enacted the role of an interested bystander. There was nothing for Zimmerman to do but take off after Collins. Zimmerman in his fastest moments couldn't spot Eddie Collins a running start and overhaul him in less than thirty yards.

Heinie Zimmerman did the best he could under the circumstances, but in effect he chased Collins across the plate with a run that some historians argue was the deciding tally in the world's series. Maybe it was a bum rap for Heinie Zimmerman, but he wasn't the first ball player, nor will he be the last, who has had to take such, and like it.

CHAPTER FOURTEEN

Though baseball was not affected noticeably through the first year of World War I—the champion White Sox played to a new seasonal high of 684,521—the game felt the full impact of disturbed world conditions in 1918.

When the "Work or Fight" order called a halt to major-league activities by Labor Day, Comiskey Park had drawn but 195,081 despite the fact that it housed such defending world champions as had not gone off to war.

The riddled White Sox were no factor in the curtailed 1918 race. They finished sixth. Comiskey Park did figure as a setting for the world's series, however, for the Cubs, winners of the National League pennant, borrowed the plant for the games with the Boston Red Sox. The capacity of the Cubs' own park would have been adequate, since the highest attendance for any of the games played in Chicago's end of the series was 27,054.

If the White Sox were no factor in the playing side of the American League's 1918 activities, they were involved in a complicated warfare with the National Commission. The outcome of this represented the final and official break between Comiskey and Ban Johnson, the American League president. Whatever had caused them to fight before was strictly minor league compared with the tempest which blew up over the disposition of the services of pitcher Jack Quinn.

Conditions brought about by the war were the direct cause of the Quinn case. He had joined the Vernon club of the Pacific Coast League in 1916, after the outlaw Federal League had folded the year before. He had been with the Baltimore club of the Federal group. The Pacific Coast League, as was the case with most of the minors, found it unwise to play out its schedule in 1918, and called a halt long before the "Work or Fight" ruling put the quietus on all baseball. All major-league clubs, still struggling to keep going, were making earnest efforts to land worth-while minor-league players for stopgap purposes, and Comiskey fancied Quinn for the White Sox.

Before entering into a detailed account of the Quinn case, it may be well to remember that from the time the American League was recognized as a major by the National, in 1903, a three-man Commission ruled over such baseball affairs as were not strictly the business of the respective leagues themselves. The National Commission, as this body was known, included the American League president and the National League president. August Garry Herrmann, owner of the Cincinnati club, acted as chairman. In 1918 Ban Johnson still ruled the American League, but John Heydler had succeeded John K. Tener as National League president in August, and thus automatically became a member of the National Commission. Herrmann still functioned as chairman.

Actually, the Quinn case had its origin before Tener's resignation, for it was in July that Comiskey pursued his first inquiry into Quinn's status. He was given permission to deal directly with the player, rather than with the Vernon club which held title to him prior to the Pacific

Coast League's blowup. Quinn came to terms with the White Sox and joined the club.

Later on it was discovered that the New York American League club was dealing with the Vernon club for the player's services on the same day Comiskey was negotiating directly with Quinn, having first obtained the Commission's sanction.

The claim of the New York club for Quinn was then brought before the National Commission. In a decision that sets some kind of a record for confused expression, the Commission ruled in favor of New York, and awarded Quinn to that club.

Since the Quinn case was the final destructive blow to any hope of a reconciliation between Comiskey and Johnson, and the hatred of one for the other had important bearing on White Sox affairs which were to affect all baseball a year later, the National Commission's transcript of the case is presented in its entirety:

In re claims of the Chicago and New York American League clubs to the services of player Quinn.

Both the Chicago and New York American League clubs claim the services of player Quinn. This case is a rather peculiar one. On July 15, 1918, Mr. Comiskey wired the Commission as follows:

What is the status of Pacific Coast League players? Have major leagues authority to deal with players direct both for balance of this season and for future? Please advise.

In reply to this telegram the Chairman of the Commission sent him the following:

Would hold any major league club has authority to deal with Pacific Coast League players or other disbanded leagues. Commission will make a definite ruling on the matter in a few days.

Subsequent to this the Commission did make a ruling which had already been agreed to some time previously to the sending of the telegrams above referred to, that when a league disbands, players who had not previously been released to other clubs could negotiate for their services with any club they cared to, and the club securing such players would be permitted to retain them for 1919 if they desired to do so upon the payment of the draft price when their names were placed on the reservation list.

Acting upon the advice of the Chairman of the Commission, Mr. Comiskey notified it on July 18 that his club had accepted terms of pitcher Quinn and wanted a record made thereof, which was done.

On the same day, namely July 18, the president of the Los Angeles club wired the Commission as follows:

> Los Angeles and Vernon clubs are playing series ordered by directors of league and until that period is complete we have right to dispose of players as we see fit.

It seems that the league itself had disbanded previous thereto. In reply to this telegram the Chairman of the Commission wired Mr. Comiskey as follows:

> Question rights of Coast clubs to sell any players now.

When Mr. Powers' claim was made that as the Los Angeles and Vernon clubs were still playing a series of games under the directions of the Directors of the Pacific Coast League, and their players were under contract, they had a right to dispose of them, Mr. Comiskey's attention was called to it through some channel and he thereupon took the matter up with the National Commission by telephone and was told to deal direct with the player and pay no attention to the owners for the present as an adjustment with the owners could be made later on if the latter had any right to the player's services.

Mr. Comiskey acted in strict accordance with the instruction of the National Commission, which at that time had no knowledge that any other club was negotiating for the player's services.

The evidence further shows that on the same day the player accepted terms with Mr. Comiskey, the New York American League club had negotiated for the player's services with the Los Angeles club direct and had accepted that club's terms for the player.

The question then arises in this case as to whether or not the Los Angeles club had a right to dispose of this player's services at the time that they did, notwithstanding the fact that Mr. Comiskey had already accepted his terms, under instructions from the Commission.

This Commission holds, after carefully reviewing all the evidence, that the Los Angeles club was within its rights in disposing of the player to the New York club at the time that they did.

This controversy is rather unfortunate for several reasons. The advice given Mr. Comiskey in the matter of the Commission was in line with the thought that was in its mind at that time, yet at the same time the advice probably would have been qualified had the Commission known that another club was negotiating for the player's release.

Unfortunately, in this case, Mr. Comiskey having followed the advice of the Commission probably may have lost the opportunity to deal direct with the club and thus may have secured the player's release previous to the time that the New York club commenced to negotiate for him.

The player is awarded to the New York American League club.

(Signed) B. B. JOHNSON, JOHN A. HEYDLER,
AUG. HERRMANN, *National Commission*
Cincinnati, August 26, 1918.

That make everything clear?

Maybe so—but all research has failed to disclose that when Comiskey vehemently protested the Johnson-dominated National Commission ruling against him, neither he nor anyone else called attention to the most glaring pair of errors ever recorded in an official baseball ruling.

The ruling reads in its closing stages, "... The question that arises in this case as to whether or not the *Los Angeles club* had a right to dispose of this player's services...." And again, "... The Commission holds, after carefully [?] reviewing all the evidence that the *Los Angeles club* was within its rights in disposing of the player to the New York club at the time that they did."

John Picus (Jack) Quinn, who went from Vernon to Chicago to New York, had about as long a service record, major and minor league, as has ever been given to a professional ball player. However, never for a moment was he the property of the Los Angeles club. But you would never guess it from the findings of baseball's best administrative minds as they functioned on this league-shaking occasion.

Such were the slipshod ways in which the National Commission did its business in the good old days.

CHAPTER FIFTEEN

THROUGHOUT the unsettled 1918 season there had been much talk and some evidence of dissension in the ranks of the White Sox. It was common knowledge that some of the cast were not on speaking terms with the others. Part of this was due to the personalities of the individuals, part was due to the wage scale. Some of the ranking players seemed to have been bad bargainers with Comiskey according to salary standards elsewhere in the league. There was a report extant that the players, while being exhorted to go all out to win the 1917 pennant, were told that they could expect sizable bonuses from Comiskey, such as he had awarded his successful 1906 club. Instead, the story went, there were not only no bonuses forthcoming, but many of the players found they had been subjected to salary cuts when contracts were sent out for the 1918 season.

There was also some feeling that Eddie Collins, highest priced player on the club, had managerial ambitions. This the great second baseman stoutly denied.

Manager Rowland, for all of the fact that he had led the team to a world's championship, was not too happy with his lot. He felt that he was getting room and board in a den of jaguars, with a hyena or two and a few wolves tossed

Charles Robertson, who on April 30, 1922, shut out Detroit 2 to 0 without allowing a man to get on base, thus pitching one of the few "perfect" games in modern major-league history. (*The Sporting News.*)

Ted Lyons, pitcher, and from 1946 through 1948 manager of the
Chicago White Sox. (*The Sporting News.*)

in for good measure. When opportunity presented itself for him to acquire a part interest in the Milwaukee club, he bowed out.

Rowland's career thereafter was a busy one. Before he was to begin functioning as the able president of the ambitious Pacific Coast League, his present post in baseball, Rowland tried his hand in minor and major leagues as owner, executive, coach, and scout. For a brief spell he served as an American League umpire. However, well known as he has become for his participation in and influence upon baseball, Rowland's greatest claim to fame in Chicago is that he was the last manager of either of its major-league clubs able to bring the city a world's championship.

When Rowland left, White Sox manager number nine, since 1900, turned up in the person of William (Kid) Gleason, a coach since 1912.

Gleason was a belligerent little man whose playing career had dated back to the horse-and-buggy days, and he was just the type to take complete charge of the club in all departments. His activity even encompassed duties ordinarily in the trainer's keeping, and the Kid was as good a man with tape and bandages, pills and ointments as he was with the quick retort. Whether the oddly assorted personalities on the club respected Gleason, feared him, or a bit of both, they did square away in the 1919 season and exceeded even their efforts of 1917 in their activity on the ball field.

They were a great ball club, defensively and at bat. They had to be to make up for a pitching deficiency that cropped up when Red Faber, the hero of the 1917 series, pulled up lame before the 1919 season was in its critical stages.

Gleason placed great reliance on Eddie Cicotte and Claude Williams, who had blossomed into a fine left-hand pitcher. In the process of development that year was another left-hander, the youngster, Dick Kerr. These three, with occasional help from bits and pieces of pitching material picked up as it floated by on the American League tide, kept the White Sox at the top, or very near to it, from start to finish of the race.

Baseball's powers had decreed that this season, the first following the war, should be of 140 games instead of the more familiar 154.

The White Sox took to the track and shook off intermittent challenges of New York, Cleveland, and Detroit, fighting all the way to cinch the pennant in the closing week. They finished up with a margin of three and one-half games over Cleveland, which in turn beat New York and Detroit to the wire.

It is rather significant that these White Sox proved themselves a durable lot. Eddie Collins and Buck Weaver played in every game, while Joe Jackson missed but one and Happy Felsch five. Ray Schalk, in the midst of establishing a record for endurance among major-league catchers for appearing in more than one hundred games each season, handled the White Sox pitchers in all but nine games of this year.

The pitching trio's record of steady employment was equally interesting. Cicotte, leading the league's pitchers with twenty-nine victories and seven defeats, appeared in forty games or 307 innings. His earned run average per game was 1.82, bettered that season only by the superlative 1.49 of Walter Johnson of Washington. Williams was in forty-one games or 297 innings, and Kerr in thirty-nine games or 212 innings. So there really wasn't much left for the rest of the staff to do, even if the rest of the staff had been capable of doing it.

The White Sox of 1919 were not only durable, but, as an examination of the record book shows, they were very good at their trade. For example, Cicotte's record in more detail showed that he had worked in thirty complete games, more than any other pitcher in the league that season. His 307 innings was also the top mark for pitching activity.

Chick Gandil, first baseman, handled 1,176 chances and made but three errors for a .997 average and a new league record. Happy Felsch in a game June 23 handled twelve chances in center field to establish a record that endured until Johnny Mostil, another White Sox center fielder, came along in 1928 to equal it. Eddie Collins led the league in stolen bases with thirty-three and the club as a whole stole 145, getting a cluster of seven in one game.

The White Sox batting average for the season was .287, high mark for both major leagues. Their batsmen fanned but 361 times in the 140 games.

Exclusive of the pitchers, the White Sox batting order produced these individual averages for the season: John Collins (who alternated in right field with Nemo Leibold) .279; Leibold .302; Eddie Collins .319; Weaver .296; Jackson .351; Felsch .275; Gandil .290; Risberg .256; Schalk .282.

Defensively the team ranked behind the Boston Red Sox with a .969 average against .975, and led the league with 122 double plays. Gandil topped all the fielding first basemen; Eddie Collins was a point behind Joe Gedeon of St. Louis among the second basemen; Weaver in ninety-seven games at third base was four points behind Oscar Vitt of the Red Sox, and in forty-three games at shortstop was topped only by Everett Scott, also of the Red Sox; Risberg in ninety-seven games at shortstop was sixth among the league's regulars. In the outfield Felsch with thirty-two assists, and Leibold with twenty-six, proved the deadly accuracy of their throwing arms, with only Babe

Ruth of Boston, twenty-six assists, and Tris Speaker of Cleveland, with twenty-five, offering a challenge.

This was the kind of a ball club Kid Gleason sent freewheeling its way through American League competition in 1919. It had a confidence in its own powers to the point of rashness. It was the sort of a club that could ask, and often did ask its pitchers, "How many runs do you want today?" and being told, more often than not went out and got them.

These White Sox are regarded by many sound observers as the greatest ever put together, but alas! they will be remembered chiefly for the unsavory odor several of their members left in the wake of the world's series. They were pronounced favorites to call their shots against the Reds. Instead they lost out in what the charitable termed the greatest "upset" in world's series history. The uncharitable (and in the light of later development the more accurate observers) regarded the outcome from the first game on as something more sinister than the overturning of the "dope."

Because this series and its aftermath provided major-league baseball with a topic that will always be discussed, it has to be treated in all its detail. This is necessary for a complete understanding of what happened, and to whom. The charges, countercharges, investigations, and such will be discussed in proper turn in the hope that the confusion will not be as it was in 1919. At that time, nearly everybody professed "to know something" but no one knew anything well enough to prove it.

CHAPTER SIXTEEN

WALTER (DUTCH) RUETHER, whose nineteen and six record was the National League's best, and whose 1.81 earned-run average compared favorably with those of Grover Alexander and Jim Vaughn of the Cubs, not only pitched but slugged his way to a 9 to 1 victory for Cincinnati in the opening game of the series. Ruether's first of a pair of triples was the deciding factor in a fourth-inning five-run rally in which the Reds knocked out Eddie Cicotte, broke a 1 to 1 tie, and set up a lead which permitted them to coast the rest of the way. Later in the game Dutch drove home another run, his third for the day, and an additional single, along with his six-hit dole to the slugging White Sox, made him the day's hero to the 30,511 present in Cincinnati.

Ruether was not the only Red batsman to take kindly to the offerings of Cicotte, and of Roy Wilkinson and Grover Lowdermilk who followed him into action. Jake Daubert, the Reds' first baseman, and Greasy Neale, their right fielder, each contributed three hits to the total of fourteen amassed by the National League champions. Edd Roush, who was to play an amazing defensive game throughout the series, came through with three spectacular catches, Happy Felsch, John Collins, and Eddie Collins being his victims.

The score was tied at 1 to 1 when the Reds came to bat in the fourth. Felsch deprived Roush of an extra base hit with a great running catch. This was Happy's return for a similar act against him by Roush in the first inning.

Pat Duncan then singled but was forced at second, Swede Risberg's slow throw preventing a double play. Earle Neale lifted a short fly over Risberg's head which the Sox shortstop just failed to handle. Ivy Wingo singled and Larry Kopf, who had forced Duncan, was able to score. Ruether then delivered his triple, accounting for two more runs, and came home himself on Maurice Rath's single. When Jake Daubert also hit safely, Cicotte was replaced by Roy Wilkinson.

A combination of hits and an error along with some sluggish infield play gave the Reds two more runs in the seventh, and the final run came over in the eighth, giving the Reds their stunning 9 to 1 victory.

Wildness on Lefty Williams' part cost the Sox the second game of the series, 4 to 2. In the fourth inning of this game a fine scoring opportunity off Slim Sallee was afforded the Sox when Buck Weaver and Joe Jackson both hit safely and Felsch sacrificed them along. However, neither Gandil nor Risberg could keep the rally alive.

In the Reds' half, Rath walked, was sacrificed along, and after Groh also walked, Roush's single scored the first run. This was the first hit Williams had allowed. Risberg's alertness broke up a projected double steal by the Reds, Roush being retired. But Williams then walked Duncan, and saw his first pitch to Kopf hit for a triple, two runs scoring.

The Sox were deprived of a run in the sixth when Weaver doubled, took third on a balk, and saw the effort wasted as Roush raced to the center field fence for Felsch's powerful drive.

In the seventh the Sox were more fortunate, Neale's wild throw permitting Risberg and Ray Schalk to score, after both had reached Sallee for hits. This brought them within two runs of a tie, the Reds having scored a routine run in their half of the sixth. But that was as close as Sallee permitted them to get.

The third game brought the series to Comiskey Park, where the Reds were helpless before the three-hit pitching of Dickie Kerr, tiny Sox left-hander, and were shut out, 3 to 0.

Ray Fisher, the first right-hander that Reds' manager, Pat Moran, had started in the series, yielded seven hits in seven innings before going out for a pinch hitter. Gandil's single drove in two Sox runs in the second inning, and Risberg's triple in the fourth went for a run when he and Schalk executed a perfect squeeze play. The attendance was 29,126 for this game.

The long-delayed Sox victory brought out a crowd of 34,363 for the next engagement, but Jimmy Ring of the Reds dashed their hopes by allowing but three hits, winning 2 to 0. Cicotte came back for the Sox in this game and allowed but five hits. However, two of those hits, combined with Cicotte's own two errors came in the fifth inning with dire results for the Sox.

There was one out when Duncan tapped to the Sox pitcher, whose throw to first was so wild Duncan went on to second. A single by Kopf put Duncan on third. Jackson, throwing the ball from left field to the plate, saw it deflected by Cicotte. The ball rolled so far away that not only did Duncan score, but Kopf went on to second. He scored on Neale's double over Jackson's head.

The Sox were now trailing in the series, one game to three, and things were getting no better, fast.

For the fifth game, Reds' manager Moran trotted out Hod Eller, the shine-ball expert, and he shut the Sox out,

5 to 0. More than that, starting with the second inning Eller fanned six men in a row, beginning with Gandil, and ranging through Risberg, Schalk, Williams, Nemo Leibold, and Eddie Collins. In the fourth inning Eller fanned Felsch only, but also threw out both Weaver and Jackson, thus being individually responsible for the retirement of the Sox line-up from top to bottom, a pitching achievement without parallel in·world's series history.

A crowd of 34,370, largest of the five games, saw Sox pitcher Williams allow the Reds but four hits. Yet he was subjected to such a bad time in the sixth inning, that four of the Reds' five runs, and three of their hits, combined with some atrocious defensive play, pretty much settled the outcome then and there.

It began when Eller's fly fell between Jackson and Felsch. Felsch picked the ball up and threw wildly to Risberg, Eller getting to third. Rath's single scored Eller. Rath was sacrificed to second and Groh walked. Felsch then played Roush's fly badly, but after a consultation, the official scorers credited Roush with a triple, two runs scoring. Duncan's sacrifice fly sent in the final run of the inning. An error by Eddie Collins started the Reds on the way to their final run of the game, which scored in the ninth inning. A walk, a sacrifice, and an infield out helped Roush around.

Little Kerr kept a flicker of hope alive for the Sox when he survived an early Red attack and lasted to win the sixth game, this one played in Cincinnati, 5 to 4.

Dutch Ruether, whose pitching and batting had accounted for the first game, failed to finish this one, though his successor, Jimmy Ring, was charged with the defeat when, in the tenth inning, Chick Gandil's single scored Buck Weaver, who had doubled.

The Reds had a four-run lead before the Sox began to roll. One run was scored in the fifth, but in the next inning three came booming over. Weaver doubled, Jackson singled, and Felsch doubled. Two runs were in and Ring replaced Ruether. Schalk's single scored Felsch with the tying run and it remained a tie ball game until Weaver and Gandil broke it up in the tenth.

Eddie Cicotte's third and last chance in the series came in the seventh game and this time Eddie was successful, winning 4 to 1. The Sox led all the way against Slim Sallee. Joe Jackson drove in a run in the first and again in the third. Happy Felsch's single with bases filled in the fifth scored Eddie Collins and Weaver. Cicotte had no one to blame but himself that the Reds scored in the sixth. Groh doubled with one out. Roush hit back to Cicotte who had a simple play at third for Groh, but elected instead to throw out Roush. Duncan then singled scoring Groh. An unusually low attendance of 13,923 was recorded.

The series wound up at Comiskey Park, with the Reds taking a weirdly wonderful 10 to 5 victory. Lefty Williams started for the Sox and was driven out in the first inning, the Reds scoring four runs on five hits. They added another off relief pitcher James in the second. Joe Jackson's home run put the Sox in the scoring column in the third, right after Ed Roush had made another of his sensational catch specialties, robbing Buck Weaver of an extra base hit. The Reds picked up a run in the fifth, and in the sixth hammered Bill James and Wilkinson for three more, getting their tenth and final tally in the eighth.

Only then did the Sox go into the action still hopefully expected of them by their fans. A cluster of four hits and an error enabled them to score four runs, but neither Eller nor any of his teammates was greatly concerned over that.

The Cincinnati Reds were the world's champions, victors in five out of eight games with what had been regarded as the strongest baseball team yet assembled.

The composite boxscore of the eight games of the ill-fated series:

REDS	G	AB	R	H	SB	SH	RBI	PO	A	E
Rath 2b	8	31	5	7	2	1	3	22	17	2
Daubert 1b	8	29	4	7	1	5	1	81	5	2
Groh 3b	8	29	6	5	. .	1	2	8	19	2
Roush cf	8	28	6	6	2	1	7	30	3	2
Duncan lf	8	26	3	7	. .	3	8	9	1	. .
Kopf ss	8	27	3	6	. .	1	3	10	29	1
Neale rf	8	28	3	10	1	. .	4	20	. .	1
Wingo c	3	7	1	4	. .	1	1	8	3	. .
Rariden c	5	19	. .	4	1	. .	2	25	3	1
Eller p	2	7	2	2	. .	. .	. .	. .	2	. .
Ruether p	3	6	2	4	. .	. .	4	. .	2	. .
Sallee p	2	4	. .	. .	. .	. .	. .	1	4	. .
Ring p	2	5	. .	. .	. .	. .	. .	1	3	. .
Luque p	2	1	. .	. .	. .	. .	. .	1	. .	. .
Fisher p	2	2	. .	1	. .	. .	. .	. .	6	1
Magee p.h.	2	2	. .	1	. .	. .	. .	. .	. .	. .
Smith p.r.	1	. .	. .	. .	. .	. .	. .	. .	. .	. .
TOTALS		251	35	64	7	13	35	216	97	12

WHITE SOX	G	AB	R	H	SB	SH	RBI	PO	A	E
Leibold rf	5	18	. .	1	1	. .	. .	5	2	. .
J. Collins rf	4	16	2	4	. .	. .	. .	5	. .	. .
E. Collins 2b	8	31	2	7	1	2	1	21	31	2
Weaver 3b	8	34	4	11	. .	. .	. .	9	18	. .
Jackson lf	8	32	5	12	. .	. .	6	16	1	. .
Felsch cf	8	26	2	5	. .	4	3	23	1	2
Gandil 1b	8	30	1	7	1	. .	4	79	2	1
Risberg ss	8	25	3	2	1	. .	1	23	30	4
Schalk c	8	23	1	7	1	. .	2	29	15	1
Lynn c	1	1	. .	. .	. .	. .	. .	1	. .	. .
Cicotte p	3	8	. .	. .	. .	. .	. .	. .	7	2
Williams p	3	5	.	1	. .	. .	. .	1	2	. .
Kerr p	2	6	. .	1	. .	1	. .	1	4	. .
Wilkinson p	2	2	. .	. .	. .	. .	. .	. .	2	. .
Lowdermilk p	1	. .	. .	. .	. .	. .	. .	. .	1	. .
James p	1	2	. .	. .	. .	. .	. .	. .	. .	. .
Mayer p	1	. .	. .	. .	. .	. .	. .	. .	. .	. .
Murphy p.h.	3	2	. .	. .	. .	. .	. .	. .	. .	. .
McMullin p.h.	2	2	. .	1	. .	. .	. .	. .	. .	. .
TOTALS		263	20	59	5	7	17	213	116	12

The individual batting averages of the White Sox regulars showed Jackson leading with .375. Next in line was Weaver .324 and Schalk .304. After these came J. Collins .250; Gandil .233; E. Collins .226; Williams .200; Felsch .192; Kerr .167; Risberg .080; Liebold .056; and Cicotte .000.

Ruether's .667 average was high for the Reds, but of those who played in all the games, Neale's .357 led. Duncan batted .269, and Roush, whose phenomenal play in the outfield featured the series, hit but .214 though driving in seven runs, one less than Duncan's eight, which was best for either club.

The composite figures on the pitchers who were credited with a victory or charged with a defeat follow:

	W	L	AB	IP	SO	BB	R	H	HB
Kerr	2	0	67	19	6	3	4	14	1
Eller	2	0	68	18	15	2	5	13	1
Ruether	1	0	49	14	1	4	5	12	0
Ring	1	1	48	14	4	6	1	7	2
Sallee	1	1	55	13⅓	2	1	6	19	0
Cicotte	1	2	79	21⅔	7	5	9	19	1
Fisher	0	1	27	7⅔	2	2	3	8	0
Williams	0	3	53	16⅓	4	8	12	12	0

The total attendance at the series was 236,928. The official receipts, excluding tax, $722,414. The White Sox club's share and the Cincinnati club's share was each $87,-156.47. Each winning Cincinnati player's share was $4,-881.55. Each Chicago player's losing share was $3,254.37. The American League and National League treasuries were both enriched by $107,755, and the National Commission drew $72,241.40.

So much for the 1919 series, for what it seemed to be to the unskeptical witnesses. What it was in reality was something else again.

CHAPTER SEVENTEEN

In retracing the sordid story of the 1919 world's series one must understand one of the axioms of the game subscribed to by baseball men of that time. That was that baseball games could not be fixed. If they could, the process would involve the inclusion of so many in the plot the secret could not be kept and resultant publicity would defeat the purpose. One man, two, or three could not handle any game-throwing assignment with reasonable certainty of success. The game is such that the proper opportunity might not come the "fixed" player's way. If it did, there was no certainty that the combined efforts of the other players might not undo any evil wrought by the derelict or derelicts. For the "sure-thing" gambler's purposes, then, there had to be other more fertile fields than baseball. At least, so they believed.

In the very early days of the game, in 1877 to be exact, four players had been dismissed by the Louisville club and forever black-listed on evidence that they had thrown games at the behest of gamblers. In more modern times, there had been occasional implications that a player here or a player there had strayed from the straight and narrow. No open accusations were ever made, no public charges brought, and the player drifted from club to club. The black-list was not brought into play at all. A club owner or manager who satisfied himself that one of his players wasn't the soul of honor was content to get rid of him. If the player caught on with someone else that was someone else's hard luck.

On the night before the 1919 world's series opened there were rumors abroad in the hotel lobbies of Cincinnati that the "fix" had been put in for the Reds to win. Practically everyone regarded this as the idle gossip which often precedes any championship event in professional sport.

No one paid too much heed to the stories. Close observers of such things did note that there was unusual evidence of open betting going on, and that an incredibly large amount of money was showing for Cincinnati, which, according to the baseball experts, figured to be very much the short ender.

One of these experts, a Chicago man, had been featuring an analysis of his own design. In it he not only presumed to tell how the series would come out, but went in for predicting runs, hits and so on, in each game. His slide rule had told him that the White Sox, according to his "dope," were a cinch.

When they fell, 9 to 1, taking a disgraceful beating in the first game, there were some concurrent incidents which caused these pioneers among the skeptics to recall the "fix" rumors they had been hearing. Specifically there was the complete reversal of pitching form by Eddie Cicotte, his league's best, and some curiously inept fielding plays, especially in the fourth inning when the Reds poured five runs across.

That night Comiskey sought out his manager, Kid Gleason, and asked him if he had noticed anything strange about the game. All the Kid was willing to concede was that his ball club, his "boys" as he called them, had been very punk.

Comiskey insisted that something was amiss, and brought up the "fix" rumors he had heard. Gleason, following the club owner's train of thought, reverted to baseball's axiom, that a ball game or a series could not be thrown.

"How do you explain the switch in betting from the White Sox to the Reds?" Comiskey wanted to know. Gleason's thought then was that "New York money," possibly on a hunch, had done so. "It would need entirely too much money to put the series in the bag," Gleason insisted. Comiskey left him on that note, but remained unconvinced.

Subsequently Comiskey and Gleason met up with John McGraw, the Giants' manager, who as an old friend of both suggested that Gleason's "boys" had looked pretty bad that afternoon.

"Have you heard anything?" queried Comiskey.

"What do you mean—anything?" McGraw wanted to know, and let it go at that.

Comiskey spent a very restless night and early next morning decided to make an issue of his suspicions. Extant in baseball then was the National Commission, whose normal function would be a consideration of such extraordinary events as these. One member, and its chairman, was August Herrmann. He owned the Cincinnati club, and was then (as usual) in the midst of staging one of the entertainments for which he was noted. Comiskey couldn't talk with him.

Another member of the Commission was Ban Johnson, the American League president. Since the Jack Quinn case of the year before there was nothing but hatred between Johnson and Comiskey.

That left the third member, John Heydler, president of the National League. It required some doing for Comiskey's pride to let him go to the rival league president, but go he did. To him he first openly voiced his thought that the game played the day before had been crooked.

Heydler, a kindly, soft-spoken man who never acted on impulse, smiled at this charge. "You're wrought up too much, Commy," he said. "You're just being a bum loser. Your team was too confident, that's all, and the Reds rushed them off their feet."

While Comiskey was with Heydler, a phone call came from Kid Gleason with the report that a known gambler was now betting great sums on the Reds at even money. Comiskey relayed this information to Heydler, who refused to believe it. His idea was that the Reds were good, but they were not *that* good. Gleason, Comiskey said, had gained his information from newspapermen, who further said that much money had been wagered by the New York gamblers before coming to Cincinnati and that was why the odds had dropped. "They must know something," argued Comiskey.

This was the situation when the second game began. Lefty Williams, one of the White Sox trio of effective hurlers, had been chosen to oppose Slim Sallee. Williams in regular season had pitched 297 innings, the equivalent of thirty-three complete games. He had averaged less than two bases on balls to a game. For three innings he was almost pitching perfection, but one Cincinnati runner, Edd Roush, getting on base through a second-inning pass. He was doubled off first when the next hitter lined savagely directly at Eddie Collins.

In the fourth inning, with the White Sox leading by one run, Williams walked the first man, who was sacrificed to second. Then came another pass. Roush's hit, the first for Cincinnati, followed, one run scoring, but some awkward base running by Roush resulted in his being tagged out. Another pass, the third for the inning, from a man who had averaged less than two to a game, followed. Another hit, this one a long triple by Kopf, sent across two more runs and gave the Reds all the runs they were to need, though they did make another later on. In the sixth inning the fifth base on balls of Williams was followed in due time by a solid base hit.

After this game some of the more skeptical sports writers were on Gleason's trail. Whatever the White Sox manager thought he kept to himself.

John McGraw, who was here, there, and everywhere during the series, was encountering on all sides the rumors of the "fix." He mentioned some of this to his long-time associate, Christy Mathewson. "Maybe it's all so much hot air," said McGraw, "but you can be sure of one thing—it will take a thousand gumshoes to prove anything."

It was bruited about that the New York gambling individual who had been attracting most of the attention was still backing the Reds before the third game. In it, the diminutive Dick Kerr strode forth and hurled a masterful shutout.

Comiskey, Gleason, and all others who had nurtured misgivings about the play of the White Sox now had their suspicions lulled. The only questionable incident had taken place in the second inning. With Gandil on second and Risberg on first, and one out, two White Sox runs already in, Schalk's sacrifice attempt bounded past Fisher, the Reds' pitcher. There was no chance to get Schalk and deprive him of a base hit, which should have filled the bases. But Gandil loafed going to third and Fisher had time to retrieve the ball and get it to Groh for a force-out. However, it had been Gandil's own hit which had driven in the two runs, so what if his failure to hustle did deprive the White Sox of a chance for a big inning?

That night, however, Gleason found Cicotte, his pitching choice for the next day, wandering about the street long after regular bedtime. This caused Gleason to wonder what was on his pitcher's mind. He was unable to get much satisfaction out of Cicotte beyond a nervous "just couldn't sleep" explanation. Nor was Gleason entirely satisfied when much later that night he espied the often mentioned New York gambler slipping out of the side door of a South Side hotel at which many of the White Sox resided.

For four innings in the next day's game Cicotte kept pace with Ring, the Reds' pitcher. In the fifth inning, with one out, Duncan hit to Cicotte, who messed up the play, then threw wildly to first, Duncan going to second. A fast ball thrown to Kopf, generally regarded as having a weakness for curve balls, resulted in a hit to left. Jackson's throw home, presumably to cut off the run, never did get to Schalk. Cicotte got in its way and deflected it, with the result that the run scored and Kopf reached second. Neale then came through with a double scoring Kopf. That represented all of the Reds' runs, two of their five hits, and all of the White Sox errors for the day.

It was after this game that Gleason first addressed himself to his ball club, breaking into the open with things he had heard. "You'd think we wasn't trying," snarled Gandil. Fred McMullin, utility man to whom had been entrusted the task of scouting the Reds several days in advance of the series, later on gave out with the threat to punch anybody in the nose who dared suggest he was in on any wrongdoing. No one else had any comment on Gleason's fiery address to his squad.

That night Gleason noticed Bill Burns, a former major-league ball player and friend of several of the White Sox, talking with the New York character who was reported to be doing all the betting. The Kid became convinced that there really was something going on which had never happened before in his time in baseball. There was more than a suspicion now of chicanery. Comiskey, very low in spirits with his ball club trailing three games to one in the series, went back to see President Heydler.

"Don't tell me that game today wasn't crooked," said Comiskey. Heydler admitted cautiously that it had looked a little strange.

"Do you want me to talk to Ban Johnson?" he asked Comiskey, who replied that somebody should do that, and without further delay.

It was Comiskey's thought that it was up to the league president to be watchful and take action. Once the idea became fixed in the public's mind that baseball wasn't being played on its merits and that no attempt was made by those in authority to check it, all confidence in the game would be lost.

Heydler reported back to Comiskey that it was Johnson's opinion that any idea of a "fix" was ridiculous. The White Sox were just victims of their own fatheadedness and the Cincinnati club happened to be red hot in the series was Johnson's curt dismissal of the idea that was bothering Comiskey, Gleason, and in a lesser degree, Heydler.

In the fifth game with Williams pitching for the White Sox, Eller's three-hit job gave Comiskey's club no chance to score. In a weird sixth inning, during which Felsch was guilty of two glaring misplays, four Red runs scored.

Gleason sent Kerr back to the mound for the sixth game. He managed to work out a 5 to 4 victory. Then it was that Cicotte went to Gleason and asked to pitch the seventh game. His request was granted and he went the route steadily to win over Sallee, and put the White Sox within one game of evening matters as the series returned to Comiskey Park.

There, in the eighth, final, and worst of all the White Sox performances, Williams was taken out in the first inning, having allowed four runs on as many hits while only one man had been retired. This commanding lead was added to, until the White Sox fell, 10 to 5. There was less to say for their all-around play in this game than there had been in the 9 to 1 rout which opened the series.

CHAPTER EIGHTEEN

SHORTLY after the close of the series, Comiskey conferred with Maclay Hoyne, State's Attorney for Cook County. The White Sox owner expressed his convictions that much had been wrong with the play of members of his club and that it was his earnest desire that a searching investigation be made.

Hoyne heard him out, and then expressed an opinion that it would be most difficult to prove a case. The only charge, he indicated, could be that of conspiracy. To get a conviction for that in Cook County it would be necessary to demonstrate to the satisfaction of a jury that the plotting had been done there. Nevertheless Comiskey insisted that he wanted a sweeping investigation. He did not care what it cost.

Meanwhile many of the newspapers were doing some broad hinting that all had not been well in the series. Ring Lardner, one of the baseball writers traveling from Cincinnati to Chicago after the first two games, went from car to car singing a parody, "I'm forever throwing ball games." But proof being lacking—and the gossip columns not being what they were to become in later years—all the newspapers were wary of the printed word.

All over the country there was discussion of the "phony" series. As the investigators, both those assigned by Comiskey and by the State's Attorney, ran down leads invariably they were disclosed to be hearsay evidence. Often it was not even clear in the hearing who said what or where it was said.

The investigators followed clues in St. Louis, in Boston, in Pittsburgh, and in New York, as well as in Chicago and Cincinnati. Some tips carried searchers as far afield as the Carolinas. Always the result was the same, little tangible, and nothing at all that would stand direct on cross-examination in a court of law.

It became known sometime after the world's series that Comiskey had held up the checks of eight members of the club. Some research disclosed that the eight were Eddie Cicotte, Claude Williams, Arnold Gandil, Charles Risberg, Joe Jackson, Oscar Felsch, George Weaver, and Fred Mc-Mullin. It was learned that some and perhaps all of these were being shadowed by investigators, but only Gandil and Cicotte had shown any signs of having come into any extraordinary lot of money.

Gandil had broken out with a new automobile, diamonds, and other marks of sudden affluence. Cicotte had lifted the mortgage on his home. The others had gone fishing, hunting, or had conducted themselves in normal fashion of ball players in the off season.

The persistent investigation found that before one of the first two games in Cincinnati Gandil had wired his wife, "I have bet my shoes." The natural inference was that he must have bet on the Reds, for at the series end he not only had shoes, but a new auto and diamonds. The result of the first two games and the series was hardly such to bring money to a White Sox backer.

Another bit of evidence—circumstantial, of course—was uncovered. It was reported that after the first game in which he was subjected to a going over by the Reds, Cicotte disdained the sympathy of a relative, saying, "I got mine!" That could also be interpreted, in the slang sense, as Cicotte's comment on the beating the Reds had given him. So it was not too important as "evidence."

After a time the players whose checks had been held up began making demands on Comiskey that he settle. He conferred with his attorney, Alfred Austrian, and was advised that under the circumstances (lack of positive proof of wrongdoing) there was nothing else to do but send out the checks, $3,254.36 to each man.

Independent of Comiskey's investigation, Ban Johnson was now pursuing a searching inquiry of his own. He had come to the conclusion that Arnold Rothstein, a notorious New York character, had been the mastermind of the "fix." The name of Abe Attell had been tossed back and forth as the "front man" in the field operations of the bettors in Cincinnati and Chicago. But again, there was no substantial proof forthcoming. A Philadelphia gambler, Billy Maharg, known to be a friend of Bill Burns, also entered the picture. Conferences involving these three were reported as having taken place prior to the series and during it, but nothing beyond that could be proven.

John McGraw, working in conjunction with President Heydler, made a detailed analysis of the play in all the series games, noting all departures from what the Giants' manager, a confirmed horse player, would probably call "true form." His findings, as passed on to Heydler, were promptly turned over to Johnson.

Thus two members of the National Commission were now busily engaged in the praiseworthy attempt of catching up with the investigation parade which had been passing Comiskey's own reviewing stand for a long time. Garry Herrmann, the Cincinnati owner, who was chairman and third member of the National Commission, was preparing to resign his portfolio as of February 11, 1920. If he had ever interested himself at all in the aftermath of the series, no public record has ever been made of it.

The winter months went on without any break in the investigations. Presently the time was at hand for the White Sox, the tried and true and the suspected, to get their contracts, sign them, and head for spring training.

Comiskey, while convinced that he had eight traitors on his reserve list, could not make up his mind to hand them unconditional releases and force the public to judge for itself why. He was to be criticized severely later on for this. Yet from his viewpoint it was asking a great deal that he cast adrift these star players, especially when the most diligent search of so many investigators had failed to come up with acceptable proof that the club had been sold out by them.

Though there were undoubtedly many who held to the opinion that certain members of the White Sox had participated in a "fix" of the series, there was enough circumstantial evidence in the records to cast doubt. Jackson, one of those who had his check held up by Comiskey, had led both clubs in batting with a .375 average and had driven in six runs. Weaver had played errorless baseball in the series and had batted .324. While he drove in no runs, only six times in the eight games, given the opportunity, had Weaver failed to advance a runner. Felsch, whose .192 average was well below par, had failed at least once in each game to move a runner along. Even he had been victimized by some brilliant Cincinnati fielding. Edd Roush several times robbed Felsch of extra base hits.

In the *Spalding Official Baseball Guide for 1920* which contained the customary world's series review, averages, and a routine account of all baseball's affairs for the 1919 season, no reference was made to any suspicion of evil influence in the world's series. On the contrary, under the heading of "Perverted Humor," the *Guide* presented, in part, this editorial:

> That it is no end of fun to try to "dope" the possibilities of the world's series, interesting to the person who undertakes it and equally interesting to the one who thinks it is all nonsense to try, must be conceded. "Dope" is a good word for it. None better, none more apropos. However, when anyone undertakes to assert that any athletic pastime which does not result according to "dope" is not fairly played, it seems that the "dope" craze has gone a little beyond the bounds of reason and, one may add, justice.

Thus did the official organ for baseball pay its respects to Hugh Fullerton, a distinguished Chicago baseball writer who had been among the first to suspect something amiss in the series, and who remained among the most persistent in striving to get proof that his suspicions were not ill founded.

Seven of the suspected White Sox duly signed to contracts for 1920 appeared for spring training, but Gandil, from the Pacific Coast, had set such a prohibitive price on his services, he was not signed and remained out of baseball.

President Johnson had served notice on his umpires to watch all activities of the White Sox during the season and report to him any suspicious conduct on the field. It is on record that only once, following a game pitched by Cicotte in St. Louis which the White Sox lost, did one of the American League umpires believe he had detected an off color incident or two. Nothing came of this.

The White Sox, great ball club that they were, progressed through the season at the top or near it, much of the way. They went into a surprising slump on a late eastern tour (a circumstance that afterward led to the suspicion that all was not well with their playing conduct once more) but in the latter part of August they were very much in the race.

Throughout the season, especially while on the road, the club was subjected to abuse from rival players and hostile fans. The insults were always about the 1919 series, and Cicotte and Williams were the targets for much of this. At home where there was certainly some general feeling that there had been a questionable situation the previous fall, the fans as represented by the outpouring at Comiskey Park showed that they were willing to accept these White Sox, for better or for worse. The paid attendance for 1920 was 833,492. This was the largest in the history of the club up to that time. It is worthy of comment that the figure was not broken until the tremendous interest in baseball all over the country in the postwar years of 1946 and 1947 established the one-two all-time records for White Sox home crowds. This latter attendance record of course was surpassed in 1951.

Late in the season, while the White Sox were engaged in a critical series at Cleveland and were apparently fighting with all their resources to regain the league lead, a new baseball sensation broke into print.

On September 4, the *Chicago Herald Examiner* broke a story of an attempt to fix a game between the Cubs and the Phillies played several days before. The story related that William Veeck, the Cubs' president, had learned of the plot and caused a switch of pitchers.

The outcome of this story was that Chief Justice Charles MacDonald ordered the Grand Jury, then in session, to make an inquiry into this baseball scandal. Charges and countercharges were being brought and the inquiry was extended to bring into the open, if possible, all that had been whispered about since the world's series of nearly a year before.

It was in the midst of this newspaper sensation that the White Sox returned from Cleveland, one game out of first place.

In Philadelphia, Jimmy Isaminger, one of the skeptical baseball writers who had viewed the flip-flop of the White Sox the previous October, sought out Maharg, the gambler who had been keeping his own counsel for nearly a year. Isaminger was persuasively eloquent and convinced Maharg that with the Chicago Grand Jury blowing the whole baseball business wide open, this was the proper time to tell what he knew. Maharg agreed.

The story which he told Isaminger was substantially as follows: In September of 1919 he was called to New York by Abe Attell and Bill Burns. He was told that his help was needed in a scheme to fix the White Sox in the event they won the American League pennant. A visit was paid to Gandil and Cicotte in a New York hotel. The players professed to be disgruntled over the low salaries they were getting after all the years they had devoted to the game. They said they could get six other players to fall in with the scheme. The price was $100,000 to be paid $20,000 before each thrown game.

Burns then sought out Arnold Rothstein at a New York race track and wanted him to put up the $100,000. Rothstein refused, but when Burns reported this setback Attell said he would give A. R. a convincing sales talk. Later on Attell said he had put the deal over, but that the money would be forthcoming after each game. It was explained that all available cash was needed for betting purposes.

The night before the first game the gamblers met with Cicotte, Gandil, and Williams, and went over the revision of the plans with respect to payment of the "fix" money.

Following the first game, Maharg went to Attell's room and saw a great amount of money. The sum of $10,000 was given to Burns for Cicotte, Attell explaining that A. R.

was a little late with the rest, he had so much tied up in the venture. Burns, who had a key to Cicotte's room, went there and put the money under a pillow.

Maharg and Burns came to the conclusion after the second game that Attell had double-crossed them and that A. R. had not been behind the plot, at all. It was Maharg's assumption that the players, finding their money not forthcoming after the second game, got sore and went out to win the third game. It was his opinion that Attell had complete knowledge of this and bet on the White Sox, for all of a show he had made of backing the Reds for the third day in a row. Maharg and Burns, not knowing until too late, had backed the Reds heavily in the third game and were big losers.

It was Maharg's final opinion that several of the players, crossed either by Attell or by one of their own coplotters, never did get any money.

The sensation this story created when Isaminger broke it may well be imagined. It came over the wires in its entirety to Chicago. Long after midnight *Herald Examiner* reporters moved in on Cicotte, waking him from sleep to tell him of Maharg's statement and question him. Cicotte denied ever having met Maharg or of knowing him, and characterized the entire statement as a lie, but he was undoubtedly a greatly disturbed person when the reporters left him.

The beginning of the end of the long series of investigations of the 1919 world's series was in sight.

CHAPTER NINETEEN

THE exact routine followed by Eddie Cicotte upon arising the morning of his impending confession seems as uncertain as was the evidence accruing from earlier gropings in the dark by a myriad of investigators. One version has it that the pitcher went direct to Comiskey. Another is that Alfred Austrian, Comiskey's attorney, sent for him and when Cicotte asked if he should talk there, he was told to go instead to the White Sox owner. A third and equally credible account is that Cicotte first sought out his manager, Kid Gleason, and talked with him. Gleason in a later session with Comiskey suggested that if he really wanted to find out what it was all about Cicotte should be sent for, as he was now ready to tell all he knew about the 1919 series.

Whatever the route or whatever the impulse which sent him on it, Cicotte came to Comiskey and told his story. The White Sox owner, shocked by the revelations that all of his earlier suspicions had been based on fact, advised Cicotte to go before the Grand Jury and retell the tale. Cicotte agreed to this, and presently three of his teammates, Joe Jackson, Claude Williams, and Oscar Felsch followed his lead and took their turns in testifying before the board of inquiry. All previously signed immunity waivers before giving their version of the fixed series of 1919. The Grand Jury hearings, of course, were in secret, but such was the sensational coverage of the event by the Chicago newspapers the streets in the vicinity of the Court House were jammed with people. Jackson, on leaving the premises after testifying, was quickly recognized by the crowd. As he pressed through it, a small boy clung to his arm and cried, "Say it isn't so, Joe!"

Jackson hung his head and walked on without a word.

After the appearance of the four White Sox players before the Grand Jury, Comiskey sent the following telegram to the eight suspected players:

> You and each of you are hereby notified of your indefinite suspension as a member of the Chicago American League baseball club.
>
> Your suspension is brought about by information which has just come to me directly involving each of you in the baseball scandal now being investigated by the present Grand Jury of Cook County resulting from the world's series of 1919.
>
> If you are innocent of all wrongdoing, you and each of you will be reinstated; if you are guilty, you will be retired from organized baseball for the rest of your lives if I can accomplish it.
>
> Until there is a finality to this investigation, it is due to the public that I take this action, even though it cost Chicago the pennant.

At the conclusion of its hearing the Grand Jury indicted the eight ball players and several gamblers.

The players immediately secured themselves a formidable squad of attorneys and prepared to fight the case. It was up for hearing a few times early in 1921, but had to be postponed for one reason or another. It finally got to trial on July 18.

Bill Burns, one of the star witnesses, had been missing for a long period but through the efforts of Ban Johnson he was finally located. He took the stand and remained on it for two days of the trial. His story was materially the same that had been related to the Philadelphia newspaperman by Billy Maharg, months before.

The much discussed Abe Attell who had appeared to be the key man in the entire incident did not appear for the trial. He avoided it by the adroit legal expedient of refusing to admit he was the Attell mentioned in the indictment. Other witnesses were heard, but the accused members of the White Sox, on advise of counsel, did not go on the stand.

When the trial began it was discovered that the confessions of Cicotte, Jackson, and Felsch made to the Grand Jury ten months before had been lost, as had the immunity waivers the players had signed. It was Ban Johnson's contention that Arnold Rothstein had negotiated the deal whereby these important papers became lost, strayed, or stolen. This made for additional sensational reporting in the public prints.

The twelve good men and true, hearing what evidence there was and much of it contradictory, reached a verdict on the night of August 2. They held the accused were not guilty of conspiracy and had committed no crime in Cook County. Before the case went to the jury the judge had instructed that there was no evidence implicating Buck Weaver.

The civil verdict of "not guilty" was just as Maclay Hoyne had pointed out to Comiskey it might well be when the question of an official investigation of the 1919 rumors first arose. The ends of baseball justice were served just the same. Not one of the eight players was reinstated, nor did there seem to be any public clamor that any of them but Weaver be returned to good standing. A petition signed by thousands of fans asked that Buck be brought back to duty with the White Sox. The petition did not get any action and Weaver remained under baseball's ban. As the only one of the black-listed eight continuously resident in Chicago, he has been considered by the rank and file of the city's baseball "Old Timers" as more sinned against than sinning.

The others, after spasmodic attempts for rehearings of their claims for salary due from Comiskey, drifted into obscurity, but they served in their own warped way as the medium through which a New Deal for all baseball was to be brought about. There arose an immediate desire by the most substantial of the club owners and executives to scrap the National Commission. Many felt its haphazard methods, if not conducive to the foul blot on the game, at least contributed to the situation which permitted the scandal sore to fester for nearly a year before something was done to alleviate it.

Perhaps one of the more telling arguments in favor of reorganization of baseball's administrative office was the blistering statement issued by Comiskey during the progress of the Cook County Grand Jury's investigation in September, 1920. It read:

> The world's series of 1919 started on the third day of October in Cincinnati. Immediately I began to hear rumors that some of my ball players had been fixed.
>
> I sent for John Heydler, president of the National League and a member of the National Commission. This was the morning of the second game.
>
> I told him of the rumors I had heard. I told Mr. Heydler I was sending for him and not for Johnson because I had no confidence in Johnson.
>
> I immediately sent for Manager Gleason. I also told

him of these rumors. I told Gleason to take out any ball player who did not appear to be doing his best.

The stories of fixing would not down. I offered a reward of $10,000 for proof of the fixing of any of my ball players.

I heard that a gambler in East St. Louis had been crossed by the gamblers and lost $5,500 on the game, and that he would tell the story of the alleged frameup if he could get his $5,500 back.

I sent Manager Gleason and another man to East St. Louis and offered to pay this man the $5,500 in question if he would give us the information, but to no avail.

I employed a large force of detectives to run down every clue and paid them over $4,000 for their services in running down every clue imaginable, but could get nothing tangible.

After the world's series I withheld for several weeks the world's series checks to my ball players whose names, rightfully or wrongfully, had been mentioned in connection with the scandal, and it was only after I could get no evidence of crookedness that I cheerfully sent the checks in question to the players of my club.

At no time since the playing of the world's series did I have any cooperation from Johnson, or any member of the National Commission, in ferreting out this charge of crookedness.

Johnson now says that an official investigation was made. If so, it was made unbeknown to me, my manager or my ball players.

The result of such an alleged investigation has never been communicated to me nor to the league.

In line with the policy I have always pursued, I have offered to the State's Attorney of Cook County and the judge of the Criminal Court who has charge of the present Grand Jury every assistance by way of money or otherwise to turn up any evidence of crookedness that exists affecting the honesty and integrity of the great American pastime—baseball.

I'll go further. If any of my players are not honest I'll fire them no matter who they are, and if I can't get honest players to fill their places I'LL CLOSE THE GATES OF THE PARK that I have spent a lifetime to build and in which in the declining years of my life I take the greatest measure of pride and pleasure.

Within a few months of the disposition of the baseball scandal, the National Commission passed out of existence. In its place arose a one-man Commissioner with supreme authority over the game. The first Commissioner was Kenesaw M. Landis, then a federal judge. His selection and the unlimited power vested in his office was hailed by all baseball as something the game needed badly at that precarious state of its existence. By all baseball, that is, save Ban Johnson. He did not care any more for Judge Landis than he did for Charles A. Comiskey, but the sands of Johnson's baseball time were running out.

CHAPTER TWENTY

ONE of the first acts of Commissioner Landis was to make binding for all time the banishment of the eight "Black Sox" from organized baseball. There perhaps the tragedy of a great baseball club should be permitted to lie. Yet there was so much of a contradictory nature in the revelations of the enormity of the offense against baseball's standards of fair play, other sets of opinions must be given, such as the reaction of the White Sox players who kept the faith. From them some interesting bits of comment have been obtained.

There was nothing of the one happy family as far as personal relations of the White Sox were concerned all the while it was together. Eddie Collins, second baseman and captain, hadn't spoken to Chick Gandil, the first baseman, for more than two years prior to the 1919 series, and there was nothing clubby about Collins' relations with Swede Risberg, the shortstop, either. Risberg in turn was at odds with catcher Ray Schalk through this same period. Neither Collins nor Schalk had much in common with outfielders Joe Jackson and Happy Felsch on the field, and none at all, off it.

It has been related that when Frank Chance's famous

Cub team of 1906–08 was in its heyday, second baseman Johnny Evers and shortstop Joe Tinker did not speak to each other. However, their animosities were never such as those which existed on the White Sox. Here was a situation in which, as he himself has said, Collins rarely got hold of the ball during infield practice maneuvers unless Schalk threw it to him.

Several of the members of this club would never be rated as mental giants, and one was not far removed from illiteracy. Claude Williams, Joe Jackson, and Happy Felsch were easily led. Years after the breakup of the team Collins regretted that he had not known of their leanings in time. He was convinced that they might have been steered as easily in the right direction as they were stampeded into misfortune.

Under Kid Gleason's distinctive method of managing these oddly assorted personalities, Collins was given more authority than is usually a field captain's portion. This was resented by the anti-Collins faction, which also brooded over the fact that he was the highest paid performer on the club. Collins was essentially a team player, for all of his distinguished record as an individual, so it occurred to him that possibly Gleason's delegation of too much authority to him was not for the club's best interests.

"Some of these fellows seem to want to do just the opposite of what I tell them," Collins argued. Gleason replied that he didn't think any captain of his would be so dumb as to be unable to figure out a countermove for that.

"If you want 'em to bunt, tell 'em to hit straightaway," said Gleason. "If you want 'em to hit and run, tell 'em to bunt. Do I have to do *all* your thinking for you?"

Since there was so little to bring these discordant groups together off the field, it is not surprising that the "rights" did not suspect there was anything wrong with the series play until Gleason himself made it the subject of discussion in a clubhouse meeting. The players' memories vary on the exact time this took place. Some say it was before the third game, others say it was after the fourth.

The second inning of the fourth game, in which Williams issued his three passes with disastrous results, presented an interesting sidelight. Schalk, catching the game, kept up a persistent fire of crisp adverse comment at the way plate umpire Billy Evans was calling the pitches. It is Evans' recollection that of the three men walked in that fatal inning, all ran the count to three and two before drawing the fourth ball. Not one of the pitches, Evans and Schalk agree, missed the plate by more than the matter of an inch or two. Were it not for the fact that each of these passes was followed by a pitch "fat" enough for a telling hit to be made off it, the entire episode might have been written off as a succession of tough breaks for the pitcher.

That appeared to be Schalk's snap judgment as he protested continuously at umpire Evans' ruling on all those close ones. Evans, one of baseball's best umpires of all time, was very patient about it. He explained to Schalk that he was sorry as hell about it, but that even though a pitch missed the plate by a fraction of an inch it still was not over and therefore was a ball.

Bill Guthrie, a less distinguished American League umpire of another day, phrased it more forcibly and more succinctly on a similar occasion when a catcher clamored for his share of the close ones. "In dis game," said umpire Guthrie, "dere are no close ones. It's either Dis or Dat !"

A tough control break for Williams, then, was all the fourth game's second inning episode meant at the time for umpire Evans and catcher Schalk, and they were the two in the best position to study it while it was unfolding. The "fat" pitches which followed were dismissed as the inevitable result of a pitcher lacking control trying to "steer" one across in an attempt to get the range, once more. When it was established, long after, that there had been evil afoot, both umpire Evans and Catcher Schalk could but marvel as they recalled Williams' demonstration. If he were "wild"—as the three bases on balls in one inning would indicate in cold figures of a boxscore—and if he were so deliberately, then he actually gave the greatest demonstration of control, i.e., putting the ball where *he* wanted it to go, that baseball has ever known.

For another reaction to this extraordinary club, it is necessary to review its record in 1920, the last season it was intact save for the absent Chick Gandil, who chose not to return after 1919. Late in the 1920 campaign when Comiskey suspended the eight offending members of the White Sox indefinitely "even though it cost Chicago the pennant," it did just that. A makeshift team was hastily put together to finish out the schedule. It just did manage to hang on for second place, barely beating out New York. It will be remembered that the White Sox trailed the ultimate pennant winning Cleveland Indians by but a single game when Eddie Cicotte's confession disrupted the entire baseball world.

These 1920 White Sox flashed four pitchers who won twenty-one games or more. Red Faber's twenty-three led. Then came Lefty Williams with twenty-two and Cicotte and Dick Kerr with twenty-one each. American League pitching records can be searched most carefully without disclosing another seasonal single club pitching performance comparable with that.

Faber's illness had kept him out of the 1919 series. It is the contention of Eddie Collins, Ray Schalk, and other qualified observers that had he been available, conspiracy or no, the White Sox must have conquered the Reds.

Nor was this sentiment with regard to the inherent quality of these White Sox restricted to a few. Die-hards from Chicago continue to this day to hail that club as the greatest that ever came along in baseball. "Why," runs some of their argument, "they were so good they nearly won the 1920 pennant when from all accounts they were actually trying to lose it. You can't get any better than that."

A similar form of reasoning has been offered in the years since 1919 as an explanation for plays above and beyond the call of duty made by several of the cast out "Black Sox" in the eight games with Cincinnati. "They were so skilled," it has been advanced, "they made the plays instinctively. After all, they were artists in baseball even if they certainly proved themselves veritable tyros in malpractice. That's why they looked good or even great when perhaps they didn't want to. They just couldn't help it."

The editorial writer of *Spalding's Guide,* whose second guess after the revelations was nearer than his first, already quoted, wrote:

> The gambler has done his worst again. He is the respecter of no game. He would as quickly buy the youth in the lot as the professional in the arena, if he could. He has tried both. He will try again. The honest ball player need have no fear of any gambler. There are thousands and thousands of honest ball players. There is another small group—they were ball players once— to be immured in the Chamber of Oblivion. There let them rest.

It might have seemed that the American League club owners who must have had some sympathy for Comiskey's plight would have steered a few players of talent to him after the breakup of his great ball club. Such was not the case. The grim "Old Roman" had to make the attempt to fight his own way back to the heights he had once scaled so proudly. He was not to make it again in his lifetime, but that was not for lack of trying.

CHAPTER TWENTY-ONE

In the years following the break up of his once formidable ball club, Charles A. Comiskey's attempts to restore the White Sox to first division acceptance were made against odds greater than were ever laid against any other major-league organization. He was confronted with the imperative need of restoring confidence in his public with regard to the club's activities. His baseball judgment taught him that the best way to do this was to assemble a contending team as quickly as possible. The obvious method was to deal with the other major-league clubs as he had done when securing the services of such as Eddie Collins, Joe Jackson, and Eddie Cicotte years before. Now, however, he met with rebuffs on all sides. He had no promising material to offer in trade. None of the other clubs were of a mind to sell to the White Sox ball players for cash. There remained only the minor leagues and the colleges to tap for prospective material. Past experience had proven these were sources not only unlikely to produce players for immediate use but uncertain for future purposes. And Comiskey was in a rush.

Perhaps it was the very urgency of his need which made these years of White Sox existence the most unsettled of any period since the club had been organized. During them no less than a half-dozen managers passed in review. Some of them were duly qualified and might have been sucessful if they had anything to manage. Others were stopgap managers at best, and through these years the public performance of the club went from bad to worse. While in their first twenty years the Sox had finished among the American League's top four, fifteen times, now they were launched on a career that was to find them logged in the second division for fifteen consecutive seasons.

The "Old Roman," whose health began failing after the "Black Sox" scandal, did not falter in his determination to try everything possible to restore his club to its former standing. Twice in this trying period he paid out sums of $100,000 or more for individual ball players in the hope they would help refashion the White Sox. His most telling demonstration of his own faith in the property was the expenditure of a vast sum of money for remodeling Comiskey Park. Its stands were double decked. Its symmetrical proportions were arranged in the manner that stands as a model for ball parks in which there are no trick fences, no artificial aids to base-hit production, and in which a player or a club, home or visiting, earns what goes into the record book.

The White Sox faced the 1921 season with but two acceptable pitchers, Red Faber and Dick Kerr, and a few other seasoned artisans, among them catcher Ray Schalk and second baseman Eddie Collins.

A young outfielder, Bibb Falk, up from the University of Texas, blossomed at once into a regular. He played in 152 games and batted .285. He was to improve on that, for when he closed his major-league career ten years later his lifetime mark was .314. A companion of Falk's in the 1921 outfield was the fading veteran, Harry Hooper, who had spent a dozen seasons with the Boston Red Sox. Through a long stretch there he had combined with Duffy Lewis and Tris Speaker to form an outfield that ranks with the most efficient on all counts that was ever assembled on one club.

Hooper and Falk gave the White Sox creditable service, as did the few holdover regular from the 1920 season, but the fill-ins let much to be desired. They simply did not have the winning touch and their seventh-place .403 finish represented the lowest average in the twenty-one years of the White Sox existence. The ineptitude of the players and the reaction of fans toward the scandal developments was such that the 1921 attendance dropped to 543,650.

The White Sox perked up a bit in 1922, had a fairly good .500 average and took fifth place in the race. Their attendance picked up to 602,860. This season saw Red Faber's tireless efforts recall the durability of Big Ed Walsh of another era. Faber worked in 353 innings or forty-three games, winning twenty-one and losing seventeen, but even this great record for a questionable club was forgotten temporarily as the country hailed the superlative one-game performance of one of the young pitchers, Charley Robertson.

His big moment came on April 30 when he shut out the Detroit Tigers, 2 to 0. He allowed no hits. He walked none. He hit none. The White Sox made no errors. No Tiger reached first base. Charley Robertson pitched a perfect game, the rarest of all baseball feats. His was but the fourth in modern baseball. Since the turn of the century, the perfect game was first produced in 1904 by Cy Young of the Boston Americans, pitching against Philadelphia. Next came one by Addie Joss of Cleveland, in 1908. The White Sox were the victims of this one.

The third perfect game got into the records on June 23, 1917, though it needed some explanatory remarks. Babe Ruth, then a Boston American pitcher, started against Washington and walked the first man. He didn't like the

124

call and made so much of it he was given the rest of the afternoon off by the umpires. Ernie Shore, with no time whatever to warm up, was rushed into action. Before he had a chance to complete the job of pitching to the next hitter, the man on base tried to steal second and was thrown out. Shore then retired twenty-six in a row, or all that faced him, and was credited with baseball's third perfect game.

Robertson's performance attracted attention. It would have attracted more were it not for the fact that American League interest this year, as in the previous one, was largely a matter of what the Babe was doing with the New York Yankees. The same Babe for whom Ernie Shore had served as a relief pitcher on that memorable June day in 1917.

In 1922 Ruth was working out the first year of a three-year contract at $52,000 a year. His salary at Boston in 1917 had been $5,000. No wonder then that the Babe and his exploits were the talk of the baseball-minded country.

Ruth and his home-run bat belong in this story of the White Sox. If the advent of Commissioner Kenesaw M. Landis had restored the public's confidence in baseball's administrative doings, it was the Ruth wallop which had furnished a new and spectacular interest for the fans and gave them something vital to mull over besides the "Black Sox" scandal. In 1921, even while the trial and error process was going on in a Chicago court, Ruth was on his way to a collection of fifty-nine home runs, exceeding—which no one then thought possible—his own mark of fifty-four in 1920.

These fifty-nine homers garnered in 1921, incidentally, have served the purpose for many years as a trick question on baseball quiz programs. He was to hit sixty in 1927 for the all-time record. He was to serve as a model for Jimmy Foxx, Hank Greenberg, Lou Gehrig, Hack Wilson, Johnny Mize, Gil Hodges, Ralph Kiner, Ted Williams, and Joe DiMaggio—other wholesalers in home runs. Most everyone knows Ruth's sixty homers are the record, but it is surprising how few, when asked who came nearest Ruth's record mark, will supply the correct answer: "Ruth himself, in 1921."

In compiling his lifetime collection of 714 home runs, Ruth first picked on a White Sox pitcher in 1919 when he hit for the circuit against Dave Danforth. The last White Sox hurler to watch one of his pitches soar out of the park on the power of Ruth's swing was Ted Lyons, reached for a homer on July 22, 1934. Lyons, a long-service pitcher with the White Sox, furnished eleven of Ruth's homers. Al Thomas was hit for ten, Red Faber for nine, and Dick Kerr for seven. Eddie Cicotte alone among the White Sox pitchers of consequence closed out his career (or had it closed out for him) without yielding one or more homers to Ruth's lifetime string.

Surely, Babe Ruth belongs in the story of the White Sox for more reasons than one. The one that will be stressed here is the sigh that escapes old-line White Sox followers who regarded Joe Jackson as the greatest natural hitter the game has ever known: "If he had remained square and lasted to swing on that lively ball they brought in for Ruth, who knows how many homers 'Shoeless' Joe would have collected?"

Who, indeed?

CHAPTER TWENTY-TWO

WHEN it became evident to Comiskey that he would get little help from American League rivals in rebuilding the shattered White Sox, the "Old Roman" looked to the high minor leagues. Willie Kamm, a brilliant young third baseman, was flourishing at San Francisco. He was being rated as a certainty to make good in the major leagues and the fans who paid tribute to him were familiar with excellent third basemen. On that same San Francisco club at various times had appeared Buck Weaver, Oscar Vitt, and Rollie Zeider, and Kamm's following was as enthusiastic about his chances as they had been over the others in their Pacific Coast League days.

The San Francisco club, owned by the triumvirate, Charles H. Strub, Charlie Graham, and George A. Putnam, was fully aware of Kamm's worth in the open market and was content to sit back and permit the bids to come in. Comiskey entered the list and he was moved by desperation. His offer of $100,000 which was finally accepted represented a record outlay for a minor-league player. However, it took the publication of photostatic copies of the check, as well as an exhibition of the cancelled original, to make some of the skeptical believe (a) that a minor-league player could be worth that much and (b) that Comiskey would pay it. After the airing given the wage scale of some of the players during the "Black Sox" hearings there had been a change of mind with many regarding Comiskey's once generally accepted free and easy way with money.

Kamm actually was a $100,000 bit of playing property and worth it, though his was to be a rough job in proving it. Memories of Buck Weaver, best third baseman of them all, still lingered at Comiskey Park. There was an immediate return on the investment in the form of increased public interest and when Kamm arrived for spring training at the Seguin, Texas, camp he attracted more attention than had been paid any minor-league graduate in years.

It did not take Kamm long to demonstrate that he was a flawless workman around third base. He was the subject of immediate rave notices by the Chicago baseball writers who watched him break in. As soon as the spring exhibition series began writers from other major-league cities joined in the clamor.

First to get on the band wagon were the New York writers assigned to the Giants camp at San Antonio, not far from Seguin. To convince them that any player was of professional caliber whose major-league habitat was not the Polo Grounds (then home site of both Giants and Yankees) took some doing. The tribe of Greater New York writers, then and now, subscribed to the philosophy of Bugs Baer that "outside New York it's all Bridgeport."

However, they maintained a lively interest in the neighboring Sox, not only because the two teams were meeting in a series of spring games, but because of the bond of friendship existing among John McGraw, his aide, Hughey Jennings, and the White Sox manager, Kid Gleason.

It was McGraw's custom to have a dinner party at camp-breaking time, each spring. The one he staged in San Antonio had as its master of ceremonies the inimitable (though many have tried) Bugs Baer. Amon G. Carter, famed Texas publisher, McGraw, Gleason, and a high-ranking bit of brass from the Army were among those on the dais. The bit of brass was renowned as an orator, and it was said that he was known as the "Firebrand of the Army." He was not, physically, a large man, as Generals go, but he had never let that throw him. He remembered Napoleon, too.

The bit of brass was assigned a seat next to Gleason, who was in a particularly boisterous mood that evening. After a time it occurred to McGraw that his old pal, Gleason, was annoying the bit of brass. He said as much to the Kid.

"Nuts," snapped Gleason. "Me and the Lieutenant are getting along swell, ain't we, Loot?"

The bit of brass there upon established the new Texas record for high dudgeon. "I, sir," he snapped, "am a full general."

"I, sir," retorted Gleason, "am a full manager. How in hell was I to know you're a general? I can't see your leggings."

Even Bugs Baer had trouble topping that one, during the rest of his Texas stay.

In due time, following convalescence from the McGraw dinner, Gleason was back on the job with his White Sox, battling the Giants day after day in the spring tour of the south. In one of those games Willie Kamm came up with the play that surpassed anything most reviewers had seen, up to that time.

The Giants had runners on first and second with none out when the batsman drove a hard bounder just inside the third base line. Kamm sped over, back-handed the ball, and stepped on third base. Without wasting a motion he whirled and threw to second for the force-out there. The second baseman, Eddie Collins, pivoted rapidly and his throw just nipped the batter at first base, completing a triple play.

A triple play started off a ground ball was sufficient to convince everybody that Kamm knew his way around as a defensive player. Whether he would hit major-league pitching was something else again. He answered with an impressive .292 for his first season, and when he left the American League after thirteen years his career average was .281. As a defensive player he takes his place with baseball's best. In eight seasons, six of them in succession while with the White Sox, he led all third basemen in fielding. In 1928 he went from June 26 to September 11 through a string of seventy-five games in a row without making an error. In that same season he made 243 put-outs for the year. Both are American League records.

It was no fault of Kamm's, any more than of Bibb Falk's, that the rebuilding process of the White Sox was not an immediate success. These two more than proved the soundness of the large expenditures bound up in them. The trouble was that Comiskey's limited scouting detail was unable to discover more like them to man the other positions on the riddled ball club.

In Kamm's first year the scouting system did uncover a player who was to take his place with the list of White Sox all-time heroes. He was Ted Lyons, who was heading for an A.B. degree at Baylor University in Texas when manager Kid Gleason dispatched catcher Ray Schalk to look the young man over. Schalk liked what he saw tremendously and thus it came about that after graduation Lyons began a memorable career with the White Sox. He was to remain with the club until the end of the 1948 season, acting as its manager in his final two years. This continuous working out of his major-league playing career with the White Sox and no other club bracketed Lyons with Big Ed Walsh and Red Faber, who had known no other major-league affiliation. Lyons, however, made it in one jump without benefit of minor-league experience, and as such he stands alone in White Sox history.

The debut of Lyons and the furtherance of the careers of Falk, Kamm, and Robertson were not enough to get the White Sox higher than seventh place in the 1923 race, and at the end of the season the heartbroken Kid Gleason gave up as manager. In looking about for a successor Comiskey thought of Frank Chance, the Peerless Leader, who had made baseball history with the Chicago Cubs in the early years of the century. Chance had tried his hand at managing the Yankees and the Red Sox after leaving the Cubs. He was a doubtful success at both, but his name still meant a great deal to Chicago and Comiskey had great respect for him as a manager and an organizer.

Chance was eager to return to the city in which he had gained his greatest fame but he was fated not to have the opportunity. Ill health forced him to abandon the plan, and the job of taking the White Sox to camp in 1924 and handling them through the season fell upon Johnny Evers, Chance's old teammate on the Cubs. Evers was temperamentally ill fitted to manage a club and did not care particularly about having it thrust upon him. The one season he served in that capacity was notable only for the beginning of a series of events which were to become a White Sox hallmark, strange departures from the norm which were ultimately to build up a tradition of "things which could happen only to the White Sox."

The first of these occurred when the club reached its training camp site at Winter Haven, Florida, and found no housing accommodations. A new hotel, which had been in the building process when the White Sox first eyed the Florida town as a prospective training center, was not ready when the club got there. It did not look as if it would be ready by the following spring, as a matter of fact.

131

Harry Grabiner, the sorely tried secretary and man of all work, spent many busy hours finding quarters for the considerable party, and eventually they were scattered all over the surrounding area. If the White Sox were off to a bad start that spring, their finish was even worse. They rested in last place at the end of the race, the first time in history the club had sunk that low.

This was the sorry state of affairs when the White Sox were preparing for the grand opening of their remodeled park in 1925. They had been outfitted in the interim with as likely a managerial prospect as had ever emerged from the ranks when Eddie Collins took up the burden. His choice as manager was a most popular one. He was then in his eleventh season with the White Sox, and his twentieth in the American League. Collins was as smart as any ball player ever gets. He was a born competitor. He was proficient in every department of the game even then at the ripe old playing age of thirty-eight. He should have taken his place among the successful managers, given a reasonable share of major-league ball players.

For two seasons he toiled at the impossible task and did succeed in lifting the club to fifth place. Partly because of his personal popularity and his driving tactics, and partly because of the remodeled park, the White Sox attendance soared in 1925 to an impressive 832,231, less than 2,000 below the Comiskey Park record for seasons prior to the introduction of night baseball.

On the artistic side, Collins' second and final year as the White Sox manager was productive of a no-hit, no-run game hurled by Ted Lyons against Boston. In the 1925 season Earl Sheely, slow-footed first baseman, but a skilled handler of baseballs, drove out forty-three doubles for a club record. But there was so little else that was encouraging, Collins saw no purpose in remaining on the job any longer. He abandoned his White Sox career as manager and as player, and returned to his first boss, Connie Mack, at Philadelphia. There he rounded out the rest of his twenty-five years as a player in the major leagues, an endurance record that has stood the test of time.

CHAPTER TWENTY-THREE

THE departure of Eddie Collins left Ray Schalk as the only one of the really great figures still with the White Sox. It was entirely in keeping with Comiskey's regard for his faithful workmen that Schalk should have his chance at managing the club. His catching record was studded with extraordinary feats of "iron-man" activity that were the more remarkable because his playing weight was never more than 155, and he functioned in an era when there was no restriction on spitball, emery ball, shine ball, and other eccentric pitching deliveries. In 1920 Schalk caught 151 games for an American League record. He turned in a dozen seasons in which he caught more than one hundred games in each. He belongs with all the catching greats, but he was no more the answer to the White Sox needs than Collins had been before. The club again finished in fifth place and when it showed no signs of improving its position, Schalk did not even bother to finish out his second year as manager. With his departure in July, 1928, White Sox managerial affairs for the next few seasons became very addled indeed.

Immediate successor to Schalk was Russell (Lena) Black-burne, one of the White Sox coaches. In his official term once more the White Sox owner turned to the Pacific Coast League for help and paid Portland the record price of $75,000 cash and the equivalent of $48,000 in ball players for shortstop Bill Cissell. A succession of great shortstops such as Roger Peckinpaugh, Dave Bancroft, Ivan Olson, and Charley Hollocher had come up from Portland in other seasons. Cissell was rated a prospect the equal of these, but somehow he never quite lived up to that promise.

Blackburne, the hurry-up manager of 1928, was retained for 1929 and thereby got to know intimately Arthur (The Great) Shires, a first baseman who had breezed in from Texas the year before and startled the baseball world by securing a flock of telling hits in his first major-league game. The major leagues were not yet ready for Dizzy Dean, but in his own brash way Shires could well have been the voice crying in the baseball wilderness that the advent of the one and only Dizzy was near at hand. Somewhat after the manner of Dean, Shires talked a great game. Somewhat after the manner of Dean, but not so sensationally or for no such sustained length of time, he was able to play a great game. It is for his extra-curricular activities that Shires belongs in the story of the White Sox.

He fancied himself a fighter on and off the field. He actually did appear in a few ring engagements, such as they were. One in which he was matched with George Trafton attracted the most attention. Trafton was a former Notre Dame football player and then a professional with the Chicago Bears. Their meeting, widely publicized, drew a packed house and was productive of a boresome series of rounds. The main action was an unprogrammed incident. A football teammate of Trafton's, as a form of criticism, punched the nose of a broadcaster who was giving the not too eagerly waiting world a description of the goings on inside the ring, and not, according to Chicago Bear ears, giving Trafton any the best of it.

While Shires was being featured as an antidote for many otherwise dull moments with the White Sox, on the other side of town the Cubs had an after-hours genius of their own in Hack Wilson, who happened to be their most productive batsman. Hack went in for an occasional joust with fans, rival players, and others, and when the size of the gates Shires' ring activities were producing was called to his attention he saw no reason for being coy about it. He was perfectly willing to fight Shires. Shires was perfectly willing to fight Wilson. James C. Mullen, Chicago's leading promoter, was perfectly willing to stage the great event.

White Sox and Cub fans were rallying to the cause, and there's no telling what might have happened if Commissioner Kenesaw M. Landis hadn't called a halt. He advised both principals in a few well-chosen words that if they were figuring on remaining in organized baseball any longer they had best give up their ring careers, then and there.

Thus ended the Shires professional career as a fighter. The remaining bouts on his record, as well as on Wilson's, were for the most part run-of-the-mill barroom brawls and such battles as honor demanded with rival players, newspapermen, and fans. It was typical of Shires that he had little regard for club law and authority. This accounted for a pair of impromptu engagements with manager Blackburne, and the second of these led to complications as strange as the punching in the nose of the broadcaster at the Shires-Trafton fight. When this second brawl between Shires and Blackburne started, Lou Barbour, the club's traveling secretary, attempted to separate them. In the tangle which ensued, Barbour bit his own thumb.

Such was the confusion which accompanied the White Sox in these cheerless years, it is not surprising that they sagged in 1929 to a .388 mark. This was a new low. They no longer had the vigorous, undivided attention of Charles A. Comiskey to his club's doings. He was placing more and more reliance on Harry Grabiner, his faithful associate, but even though broken in health the stubborn "Old Roman" still insisted on having the final say.

Grabiner now began to experience the first of a long stretch of years that would have caused a less faithful workman to abandon his task as hopeless. Actually it was hopeless, but Grabiner would not concede this to be so. For him each new season with its turnover of new players was approached as the one in which his beloved White Sox would come back to the greatness that had once been theirs.

In his limited executive capacity Grabiner either felt it was incumbent on him to take program from the failing Comiskey, or was so ordered. Either way suited Grabiner, for what Comiskey said had been his law in all the years of their long association. The nature of Comiskey's illness did not always qualify him for snap judgment on White Sox affairs, so Grabiner had to take the fall for the whole situation.

Blackburne in a season and a half established that he was not the answer to the White Sox problem. He was succeeded in 1930 by Donie Bush, who had been a great shortstop with Detroit, and who served managerial terms at Washington and at Pittsburgh. Bush survived two seasons, this being about par for the course, but under his direction the Sox failed to better the seventh-place finish for 1930 and wound up last in 1931.

If he is remembered at all in the long line of White Sox leaders it will be because during his term Luke Appling checked in from Atlanta. Luke was to be one of a very select company, such as Ed Walsh, Ray Schalk, Red Faber, and Ted Lyons, who stopped, looked, listened, and liked Comiskey Park (and vice versa) and stayed on indefinitely.

In all their history the White Sox had been able to furnish pitching champions, base running and fielding leaders, and as a group they had gained two world's championships in three attempts. But in all their thirty years they had never gazed upon an American League batting champion of their own. They had one now in the making in Luke Appling, though they didn't appreciate it when he moved in amid the motley crew of survivors of the ten most dismal years of White Sox history.

CHAPTER TWENTY-FOUR

THE year 1931 was a memorable one, not only for the White Sox but for the entire American League which had been brought into being through the efforts of Comiskey and Ban Johnson.

Bitterly opposing Comiskey to the last and equally hostile to Commissioner Landis, Johnson had been retired by the league as president in 1927, when his health failed. He was succeeded by Ernest S. Bernard of Cleveland. On March 27, 1931, Bernard died suddenly. Twenty-four hours later, Johnson, resident in St. Louis since his retirement, also died.

Into the vacancy created by the death of President Bernard stepped William Harridge. He had been concerned in the league's affairs since 1911 when he was first employed as a secretary by Johnson. At the time of Bernard's death, Harridge was serving as the league's secretary. He retained that office and became both president and treasurer on May 27, 1931.

With all due respect for Johnson's spectacular record as an organizer and a league executive, no period of the American League's history has been better served than the years encompassed in Harridge's rule. With his advent came better understanding and complete co-operation with the Commissioner's office and with the National League.

There was not much change in the White Sox playing fortunes this year. A few adjustments in the team were made by manager Bush, the most important being a mid-season trade of Willie Kamm to Cleveland for Lew Fonseca, whose .369 average topped American League hitters in 1929. Lou Barbour, the traveling secretary, was replaced by Joe Barry. The White Sox were decidedly no factor in the American League race. They wound up last with a .366 average. They had been last before but the .366 average was something new, even for them. Attendance which had dropped below the 500,000 mark in 1928 for the first time in thirteen years (excluding the war-curtailed 1918 season) now touched 403,550, lowest mark since Comiskey Park was built in 1910.

On October 26 of this sad year Charles A. Comiskey, founder of the dynasty, passed away after his long illness. In spite of the low state of his club in his declining years, the "Old Roman" had left his mark on baseball. He was among the first whose memory was to be cherished in Baseball's Hall of Fame at Cooperstown.

It was a strange coincidence that he and Johnson who had begun their American League careers together, who had actually founded it and worked tirelessly that it might gain pre-eminence in baseball, should both be taken by death in the selfsame year. Many of those who were left to mourn them grieved the more that they had passed on without a reconciliation having been effected.

Ownership and direction of the White Sox went to Comiskey's only son, J. Louis Comiskey. He was not too well versed in baseball's complicated processes, and was plagued by ill health. However, there remained Harry Grabiner, the faithful steward, for all practical purposes and some of

140

the impractical. These last were not more the rule rather than the exception in White Sox affairs.

Management of the ball club for the year 1932, Lou Comiskey's first as president, was given to Fonseca, lately arrived from Cleveland. It is improbable if the White Sox before or since were ever outfitted with a quainter collection of baseball's "humpty dumptys" than those to which Fonseca fell heir. Making progress with them was a physical impossibility. At the end of the season they had succeeded in losing 102 games, a White Sox mark that might endure forever. Their .325 percentage also struck the bottom of their all-time seasonal ratings. Of even more importance was the astounding drop in attendance, only 233,198 choosing to pay for what Comiskey Park served that year in the guise of major-league baseball.

One of Fonseca's problem children was Smead Jolley, who had come up from the Pacific Coast League heralded as a batsman of great prowess. It was as one of baseball's most ludicrous defensive players that he appealed to White Sox fans. The way of Jolley with a fly ball or a drive hit along the ground in the outfield was really something. In desperation, Fonseca tried to make a catcher out of Jolley, in order to get him somewhere in the line-up where Smead (and his potential batting strength) might be less likely to be ruined by a flying or bounding baseball.

The noble experiment was abandoned, Fonseca said, because sporting goods manufacturers had not yet designed a mask that would cover the top of the head as well as the face. In plotting the experiment Fonseca had forgotten the time might arise when a catcher would be required to get under a rapidly descending foul fly. Jolley was as allergic to a dropping fly as he was to a line drive.

Lou Comiskey, who liked his laughs as much as the next one, and who was as royal a host to his friends as his father had been before him, failed to get much enjoyment out of the miserable 1932 season. There is no way of telling what the size of the Comiskey bank roll was after a succession of lean years, of which 1932 was the leanest, but Lou was willing to make a deal, whatever the cost, in an effort to restore his ball club to something of the status it once held.

It so happened that Connie Mack's Athletics, rated for the three previous seasons as baseball's best, had reached that point in their existence in which the owner-manager chose to break them up.

With $150,000 to offer, Lou Comiskey purchased from the Athletics third baseman Jimmy Dykes and outfielders Al Simmons and George (Mule) Haas. This deal was to have its effect on Comiskey Park's baseball standards for many years to come. Its immediate result was to stimulate interest in the White Sox doings, and on all sides Lou Comiskey was being hailed as a worthy successor to his illustrious sire. The Athletic trio's first full season with the White Sox did succeed in lifting the club to sixth place, and the attendance rose to 397,789. The traditionally loyal fans were coming out of their hiding places, but there were too many of them yet concealed to give much comfort to Lou Comiskey.

The year 1933 that saw Dykes and his two Athletic associates reach Comiskey Park was the one in which a new honor was conferred on this historic baseball edifice. Arch Ward, the sports editor of the *Chicago Tribune,* put into execution this year the first of the All Star Games, which pitted a popular selection of the American League's best against the National's. Comiskey Park was chosen for the inaugural of this event which was to become a standard midseason major-league feature.

The American League side, directed by Connie Mack,

142

took the ball game, 4 to 2, from the National League group managed by John McGraw.

Simmons and Dykes of the White Sox were in the American League starting line-up and played through the entire game, Dykes being one of the two American Leaguers collecting more than one hit off National League pitching. The other to get two hits was Babe Ruth. He made the All Star Game official by hoisting a homer into the right-field stands in the third inning, scoring Charley Gehringer of the Tigers ahead of him. Dykes scored the American League's first run, getting home on a single by Lefty Gomez of the Yankees, who confessed afterward that he could never remember any previous occasion on which he had ever made a hit, much less had driven in the first run of what seeemd to be a very important ball game.

Though there was an All Star Game at Comiskey Park, and a sudden uplift in White Sox fortunes in 1933, the next season held no such bright features.

Affairs of the club went from bad to worse, and as is usually the system with baseball clubs and those of Chicago in particular the situation seemed to call for a change in managers. On May 9, which was near enough to the season's start to make many wonder why he had come out for the bell at all, Fonseca threw in the towel, and the next White Sox manager was Jimmy Dykes.

In order of succession Dykes was No. 17 in the club's thirty-three years of existence. He was to last for a longer period than any of those who had preceded him. When the final count is in, allowing for what the others had in the way of material and he hadn't, the White Sox managerial career of Jimmy Dykes will compare favorably with those of Fielder Jones, Jimmy Callahan, Clarence Rowland, and Kid Gleason, to name those predecessors who remained on the job for any appreciable amount of time.

He was no miracle man in the months that were left of the 1934 race. The White Sox took over last place, winning but fifty-three games. Their attendance record of 236,559 was proof enough that when Dykes began the 1935 season, his first full year as manager, he was coming in at the very bottom.

CHAPTER TWENTY-FIVE

AMONG those on whom the critical finger could not be put when the White Sox lapsed into last place in 1934 was the new first baseman, Henry (Zeke) Bonura, who had foresworn the banana business in New Orleans for baseball, and who came up for major-league scrutiny after a spell at Dallas. Zeke remained with the White Sox four seasons. When he left, being the sort who puzzled over such things, he was wondering what a first baseman had to do to hold a job with Dykes, the outspoken little round man who was then in charge.

In his first season Zeke hit .302 and drove in 110 runs. He hammered out twenty-seven home runs, which was a new course record for White Sox batsmen to stand from the time of the "Hitless Wonders" right on down to the year 1950, when Gus Zernial, a sort of Bonura among the outfielders, was to lift the mark to twenty-nine. In 1935 Zeke fired and fell back a bit, averaging .295 and driving in ninety-two runs. In 1936 he drove in 138 runs—the all-time White Sox record—and batted .330. His last season with the White Sox, 1937, furnished his highest batting average of all, .345, and he drove in a hundred runs.

Bonura, first baseman in an infield which had Jackie

Hayes at second, Luke Appling at short, and Dykes himself at third, was no gazelle in the field or on the bases. But in 1936 his was the distinction of leading the American League's first basemen in fielding when he made but seven errors in 1,614 chances. Bonura defensive standards being what they were, his critics had a hard time explaining this away. Their best rebuttal was that you can't miss what you don't get to.

Dykes contended that Bonura had the faculty of just failing to come up with drives that went past him for hits, which a more agile first baseman would have handled. Zeke often got where the ball had just been and made such a great flourish as it went by the expression "The Bonura Salute," coined by Ed Burns of the *Chicago Tribune*, became a part of White Sox baseball lore.

The sharp spoken Dykes once said it was a pity that in Zeke's early playing days he had not been hit between the eyes with a line drive.

"Zeke would have found out," said Dykes, "you can't get killed with a batted ball. If he had only learned that early, there's no telling how great he might have been."

Later in Bonura's career, he served the New York Giants, managed then by Bill Terry, one of the game's great first basemen in his playing days. After a brief observation. Terry was not only willing to second Dykes' motion, but argued that any further discussion be eliminated.

Bonura's first year with the Sox was noted for his hitting into three double plays in a game on May 11. That was before the big boy from the Deep South found himself. Dykes, at the time, allowed that Zeke was waiting for warm weather.

It was well that Dykes, by nature, had a great sense of humor, for in his time with the White Sox, the character actors often took the play away from the straight men.

146

One such was Frenchy Bordagaray, who appeared briefly during the 1934 season. In appearance, Frenchy looked like something left over from a Mack Sennett silent film, except that there was nothing silent about Bordagaray. Dykes took one quick look at him and sent him away. That was probably a mistake. Frenchy came back to add greatly to the diversions of the major-league scene at Brooklyn and elsewhere.

His playing record was not remarkable, but many of his other exploits were. He will be best remembered as the modern player who made an earnest effort to bring back to baseball the walrus-type mustache which was prevalent in the gay nineties.

In this same 1934 crop, came pitcher Vernon Kennedy, from Oklahoma City. He showed enough to be retained for the 1935 season. In his first complete year Kennedy broke even in twenty-two games, but one of his efforts was a no bitter hurled against Cleveland. Apart from his pitching skill, Kennedy gained further attention when a reporter revealed that he shunned hotel or apartment life to live in a trailer.

Rip Radcliff, an outfielder viewed briefly in 1934, came back to stay quite a while, beginning with the 1935 season. He was joined late in the year by Mike Kreevich, who was to take his place with the great defensive outfielders in White Sox history, sharing that distinction with Oscar Felsch and Johnny Mostil.

Radcliff is placed among Dykes' character actors by Jimmy Gallagher, now the Chicago Cubs' general manager, but then a noted baseball writer. Gallagher styles Radcliff as baseball's greatest self-defense outfielder, and points to an incident in the Yankee Stadium to make his case.

There is a sort of terrace leading up toward the lower stand of the Stadium in right field. The barrier is not too high and frequently players make efforts to snare flies that threaten to barely reach the stand. One such, a high fly, went soaring out Radcliff's way. Rip tore up the terrace, but suddenly one of his spikes caught, and he suddenly sat down with a thud. At the moment, self-preservation was Radcliff's uppermost thought. As a protective measure he put his gloved hand over his head. The descending ball hit in it and stuck for the put-out.

Nothing like that had been seen in baseball since a memorable afternoon in quaint Baker Bowl in Philadelphia when a National League outfielder, who shall be nameless, twice stumbled on the rough terrain, twice sprawled on his back, and twice was hit in the chest by the descending baseball.

"My man," says Gallagher, "caught the ball. The *ball*," he corrects advocates of the Baker Bowl hero, "caught your man."

Present and partly accounted for in this 1934–35 stretch was another brilliant fielding genius, a native Chicagoan, Jocko Conlan. Since 1941 he has ranked high among the National League's umpires, being the only playing member of the White Sox who ever took up that phase of the game. In his time away from baseball, Conlan is a Chicago florist. As an umpire-florist Jocko is no pioneer.

Many years before him, two other Chicagoans, also attached to Will Harridge's staff of umpires, decided to open a florist shop in the Loop. They were Brick Owen and Bill Guthrie, both huge men, while Conlan is on the diminutive side.

The Owen-Guthrie shop did well as long as Guthrie remained a silent partner. When Bill, who was strictly Back of the Yards, answered the phone, complications invariably set in. One fall afternoon, one of the shop's best customers, a lady who was getting ready to root for dear old Northwestern the following Saturday, phoned to inquire about a corsage of mums. Guthrie accepted the call. "What kind Mumm's we got?" answered Guthrie. "Only the best, girlie, only the best. Mumm's Extra Dry."

Along the White Sox way during 1935 catcher Luke Sewell was acquired from the Browns. This was the first of many deals Dykes was to make. He had a flair for accepting apparent outmoded material and making it shine like new for a while, at least. Sewell was a great help to the White Sox for the four years he remained with them and this despite the fact that he had been a major-league catcher for fourteen years at Cleveland and Washington before he reached Chicago. He had no service record at St. Louis. He went there on a trade for pitcher Bump Hadley and paused only long enough to be sold to the White Sox. He returned to St. Louis nine years later and steered the club to the only American League championship it ever owned.

The closing weeks of 1935 saw the arrival of pitcher Monte Stratton at Comiskey Park. He did not hit his full stride until 1937. The brilliant career forecast for him came to a shocking end in the winter of 1938 when he accidentally shot himself in the leg while hunting, necessitating an amputation. Again, that was something that could happen only to the White Sox!

By contrast with their woeful showing the season before, the White Sox fared well on the field and financially in the 1935 season. They finished but a few points behind the .500 mark and took fifth place. Their home attendance almost doubled from the previous year.

At the close of this season Dykes, in order to pave the way for some more deals, agreed to the sale of Al Simmons to the Detroit Tigers for $75,000. That was one half what Lou Comiskey had paid to Connie Mack a few years before for Dykes, Mule Haas, and Simmons.

Though they readjusted the contours of Comiskey Park to give him a better chance for distance hitting, in the three years Simmons was with the White Sox he was not the home-run producer he had been with the Athletics. He batted .331 his first year, rose to .344 the next, but had dropped to .267 when he was sold to the Tigers. In his first two seasons Simmons drove in 119 and 104 runs, for all of the fact that his eighteen homers was his highest output with the club.

Dykes was always on the lookout for castoffs from the other American League clubs and continued to show an uncanny skill in getting excellent service out of many of them. During 1936 he was able to secure pitcher Bill Dietrich from Washington and pitcher Clint Brown from Cleveland. Neither represented a great outlay of funds. Brown developed into one of baseball's most efficient relief pitchers and by the time the 1939 season was reached he was able to break the existing major-league record by finishing up fifty-six games.

The 1936 White Sox showed more energy and displayed more power than any other collection since the 1917–20 organization. They hit seventy-four home runs for a club total which was an all-time high. Appling, the shortstop who was completely relaxed at all times, winning or losing, came through with a .388 batting average, and along the way batted safely in twenty-seven consecutive games which is the club's record, as is Luke's .388 seasonal mark.

This was the American League's best for the season, so that after a thirty-six-year search the White Sox had found at last one of their members who could lead the league in batting. Appling also drove in 128 runs, which was a remarkable feat for him. While he kept his batting average well over .300 throughout his career and led the league for a second time with a .328 mark in 1943, driving in runs proportionate to his average and his place in the batting order was something Appling never regarded as his specialty.

In May of this 1936 season Dykes reached out for Fred (Dixie) Walker, who had been the property of the New York Yankees but found it too much of a task to get a place in the outfield of a club which was heading for a championship with such garden patrols as Joe DiMaggio, George Selkirk, Jake Powell, Roy Johnson, and Bob Seeds. Dixie did not see much action in 1936, but he was part of the club which wound up in third place, highest the White Sox had finished since 1920.

This sort of spirited play established Dykes as a manager and it augured well for 1937, but the Comiskey Park counting house noted with regret that its third-place team of 1936 drew 30,000 less than had the fifth-place club of 1935. That was another of those things, people said, which could happen only to the White Sox.

The chances are that their followers were not ready to believe that a good baseball club had come again to Comiskey Park after the long string of disappointments, but when Dykes, the "old-clothesman," picked up another useful pitcher in Thornton Lee, more and more people began to pay attention. The deal that brought Lee to the White Sox was a complicated one. Dykes sent pitcher Jack Salveson to Washington. The Senators in turn sent pitcher Earl Whitehill to Cleveland, and Lee went from Cleveland to Chicago. He had a most ordinary record at Cleveland but he turned in a twelve and ten record for the White Sox in 1937.

Bill Dietrich, another of Dykes' hurlers who had been undergoing the rehabilitation process since midseason the year before, burst forth with a no-hit, no-run game against St. Louis on June 1.

Monte Stratton came into his own with a splendid fifteen and five record, and some fine pitching was turned in by Ted Lyons and Vernon Kennedy, who won twenty-one games. These White Sox hurlers were responding to the treatment of coach Herold (Muddy) Ruel, who went about his work quietly. Dykes, though he played the showman on and off the field, was content to let the able Ruel get them ready.

One of the younger set in Ruel's schooling list was the husky John Dungan Rigney, a product of Chicago's own, who had been brought in from St. Paul. No one paid too much attention to him in 1937, which was a mistake. This same Rigney was to loom large in White Sox affairs in subsequent years, not only as a pitcher but as a vital factor in a front office that one day was going to get more sport-page treatment than the plays and the players. Before his pitching days were over, Rigney was to woo and win Dorothy, eldest of Lou Comiskey's three children, and present one more situation that could happen only to the White Sox.

In 1937, however, Dunc Rigney was more concerned in wanting to win some ball games, but the soft-spoken Ruel was unable to turn out a polishing job that quickly. Rigney's part was negligible in the third-place finish of the White Sox, twenty-two percentage points higher than their mark in 1936. The attendance soared to 589,245, the first time it passed the half-million mark in ten years.

CHAPTER TWENTY-SIX

Two months after the 1937 season closed Dykes engineered one of the seemingly most important swaps of his David Harum career. He sent three of his regulars, Dixie Walker, Vernon Kennedy, and Tony Piet to Detroit for Gerald Walker, Marvin Owen, and Mike Tresh.

Dixie Walker had played in every game that year. He had batted .302 and driven in ninety-five runs. Kennedy showed a forty-six and twenty-five four-year mark, including a no-hit, no-run game. Therefore, Dykes must have wanted badly one, two, or all three of the players Detroit was willing to offer, to trade Walker and Kennedy away.

The White Sox manager must have been psychic, indeed, if Tresh were the one he sought. Mike had yet to catch a ball game in the major league, and was to work in but ten for the White Sox in 1938 before he was sent to Buffalo for more seasoning.

Dykes had about reached the end of his own playing career in 1937 and Owen was a presentable third baseman. Piet was a run-of-the-mill ball player and an infielding odd-jobman.

Gerald Walker was something else again. He had been a source of great satisfaction to Detroit fans as an outfielder in two championship seasons. He was an unpredictable ball player, possessed of many of the attributes that make for the thing called "color" in an athlete. He remained with the White Sox for two seasons. In each he failed to capture the fancy of Comiskey Park fans as he had of those in Briggs Stadium. Along the way he also failed to recapture the batting and run producing strength he displayed under the Detroit banner, but he was the same wild runner around the bases he always had been.

Owen was the White Sox third baseman for but two seasons. In the second he appeared in less than sixty games, and was then sold to Boston.

Now for the other side of the trade. Piet created no more furor in Detroit than he had in Chicago. Kennedy was hardly the sort to make Tiger fans think another Wild Bill Donovan or a George Mullin had joined up. Dixie Walker kept his average above .300 through 127 games in 1938, and even though an injury cramped his style, he was hitting .305 in forty-three games of 1939 when the Brooklyn Dodgers claimed and got him at the waiver price.

Dixie was then approaching twenty-nine. He had been in baseball for eleven years, the first seven of them depositing him temporarily with as many as three minor-league clubs in a season. Strangely enough, wherever he lit or for how long, his record was always impressive, but he seemed destined to be a baseball nomad until the Dodgers put their brand on him. At Ebbets Field Dixie Walker became the "People's Choice," a hero among heroes. He carried Dodger standards through so many of Brooklyn's battles that when following the 1947 season he was transferred to Pittsburgh, the howling at Branch Rickey, the Brooklyn trademaker, was long, loud, and most pointed.

It will always be a source of wonderment to Comiskey Park fans what might have been their lot if that remark-

Luke Appling, White Sox all-time-great shortstop and only member of the club to lead the American League in hitting, 1936 and 1943. (*Chicago Herald American Photo.*)

Jimmy Dykes, White Sox manager, 1934-1946. (*The Sporting News.*)

able effort of Dixie in 1937, his first and only complete season in Chicago, had persuaded Dykes to use someone else for trading bait, no matter how much he craved the excitement which followed Gerry Walker's antics on the base paths, or how badly Marv Owen was needed for the third-base spot about to be vacated by the White Sox manager.

It might be gathered that the Brooklyn Dodgers, who were entirely innocent bystanders at the time, were the only ones to profit from Dykes' three for three trade in the winter of 1937.

They weren't. The youthful Tresh, entirely lost in the shuffle when the deal was made, was to return to Comiskey Park in 1939 and take charge of the catching. The White Sox fans would one day discuss him in the same breath with Ray Schalk and Billy Sullivan, the two who were the beginning and end of all catching if you asked for White Sox fan opinion. Or even if you didn't ask.

If Dykes foresaw that about Tresh and did not foresee what the future held for Dixie Walker, the man he let get away, then his average in the Soothsaying League has to be .500, regardless of Jimmy's own private estimate of it.

Dykes made another trade before he was ready to start the 1938 season, and this one caused almost as much excitement around Comiskey Park as had the Detroit deal of a few months before.

Zeke Bonura, who was assumed to be going steady with the first-base job, was swapped to Washington for Joe Kuhel, the fanciest handler of baseballs the White Sox has seen around first base since the days of Jiggs Donohue of the "Hitless Wonders." Kuhel's dexterity extended beyond baseball into other realms of legerdemain. He was an accomplished sleight of hand performer, and mystified one and all by making things appear and disappear.

White Sox fans enjoyed his poise, his personality, and his

performance, but it was not until the 1939 season when he made twenty-seven baseballs disappear over various American League fences that Dykes was really forgiven by his public for trading away the burly, bat-swinging Bonura. Kuhel's twenty-seven homers tied the White Sox mark that had been Zeke's since 1934, and so skilled a defensive workman was the new first-base custodian, in time that Bonura incident was forgotten. Some of the late-arriving White Sox fans, hearing tales of Zeke, are apt to say, "Bonura? Oh, yes, you mean that big guy who played first for the New York Giants for a while."

Dykes was rather pleased with the outlook for 1938 until one afternoon in Los Angeles during a spring exhibition game with the Cubs when Luke Appling, the club's most formidable hitter, slid into a base and broke his ankle. The season was almost half over before Appling was able to resume his place in the line-up. Dykes had a most promising ball club that year, but the 1938 White Sox or any other club could not have a player of Appling's status out of action for seventy-three games and make much progress. For the first time since Dykes had a complete season in which to operate, the White Sox failed to get into the first division. They finished in sixth place. Such was their lack of appeal to their following that but 338,278 came out to see them play.

They had now added a new touch to the "it could happen only to the White Sox" tradition. Their luck with weather for home games was atrocious, and it always seemed to rain hardest on Sundays and holidays when patrons in goodly numbers were certain to come out. There were even occasions on which the heavens opened after the crowd was already in the park. A rained-out Sunday or holiday is something no amount of weekday double-headers later on will balance.

If Dykes and the Comiskey ownership felt badly about

the adverse luck with which the season began and progressed, they were aghast when the news reached them of the hunting accident which deprived them of Monte Stratton's pitching service. Equipped with an artificial leg, Stratton did return to the White Sox and made a praiseworthy attempt to prove that he might be able to pitch despite his handicap. When the experiment failed he was retained as a coach for a time, and remained in the organization for a time after that.

His story was the subject of a motion picture made during 1948. In it, Dykes, who always did have a flair for the theatrical, played a part. Oddly enough, motion-picture casting being what it is, he enacted the role of Jimmy Dykes, the White Sox manager. He was letter and screen perfect in the part, too, though his White Sox managing career had ended more than two years before.

In the somewhat dismal 1938 season two of the many White Sox comets forever whizzing through Comiskey Park came up with exploits that made them one-day sensations, at least.

On June 22 Henry Steinbacher, a piecework outfielder, banged out six successive hits. In a game on September 17, when Dykes was already planning for next year (an old White Sox September custom) Mervyn Connors, reputed to be a third baseman, slugged out three home runs in one game. As far as research discloses all that this did for Connors was to give him the distinction of having hit in one game as many homers as Fielder Jones' whole squad of White Sox of 1908 had made in an entire season.

The White Sox were on the upgrade again in 1939. Before the season began Lou Comiskey recognized the value of Harry Grabiner by making him vice president of the organization, and actually its ruling head for Lou Comiskey's health no longer permitted him to take an active part in baseball affairs. Grabiner kept right on doing the same work in which he had been engaged for years. That was practically everything there was to do in administrating the business of a major-league club. He was at once the vice president, the cabinet, and all the ambassadors—which was just the way Lou Comiskey wanted it.

In this season the White Sox rose to fourth place. This was the year in which Clint Brown set his record of coming to the aid of the pitching party fifty-six times. It was also the year in which Dykes claimed pudgy Edgar Smith from Philadelphia by the waiver route. Smith responded to the Muddy Ruel treatment as so many castoff pitchers had before him. Within two seasons he was regarded as a left-hander who had all any pitcher needed save a good break, now and then. The number of 1 to 0 and 2 to 1 games in which rotund Edgar got himself involved only to be charged with defeat were enough to dampen the spirits of any less competitive ball player.

Smith remained a White Sox pitcher for several years, and in 1941 he was named for the American League All Star squad which faced the Nationals at Detroit. He was the pitcher of record when the Americans faced Claude Passeau of the Cubs in the last of the ninth, trailing 5 to 3.

Ken Keltner of Cleveland batted for Smith, with one out, and was safe on a scratch hit. Joe Gordon of the Yankees singled to right and a walk to Cecil Travis of Washington filled the bases. Joe DiMaggio of the Yankees forced Travis, Keltner scoring. That brought up Ted Williams of Boston, whom Passeau had fanned the inning before. This time Ted saw the count reach two balls and one strike and then blooie! High against the upper deck of the right-field stands crashed the ball. In came three runs and the ball game, and as Gordon, DiMaggio, and Williams crossed the plate, pudgy Edgar Smith put credit for an All Star game victory in his book of memories.

As the voluble Jimmy Dykes explained it afterward, "It

couldn't have happened otherwise. After all, at that stage of the game it was Smith against Passeau, White Sox against Cubs. And you know what always happens when they meet."

If you don't, the history of White Sox and Cub meetings, through one world's and twenty-five city series, reveals that the White Sox won nineteen series, the Cubs six, and one was tied. Of the 160 games involved, the White Sox won ninety-six, the Cubs sixty-two, and two were tied.

The White Sox–Cubs meetings as a post-season attraction were abandoned after 1942, when the White Sox had won eight series in a row, six of them while Dykes was in the driver's seat.

Dykes, the trade maker, put over two more deals at the end of the 1939 season, both affecting his outfield. He sent Rip Radcliff to St. Louis for Moose Solters, and Gerry Walker went to Washington for Taft Wright and Pete Appleton, a pitcher. Solters was the type who threatened to become a distance hitter, but he vanished from the major-league scene without having made good the threat. Wright moved right in to become a White Sox outfield fixture for nearly ten seasons.

The race the White Sox made this year was no better and no worse than that of 1939. Fourth place was again their portion. They did, however, uncover a third baseman of promise in the young Chicagoan, Bob Kennedy, who played in every one of the 154 games.

This 1940 season did get off to a start such as no other portion of a baseball race in history ever did. On opening day Bob Feller, the Cleveland boy wonder, set the White Sox down 1 to 0, allowing them no hits. That could happen only to the White Sox. Need you be advised that Feller's opponent was luckless Edgar Smith?

CHAPTER TWENTY-SEVEN

ON July 18, 1940, J. Louis Comiskey died. Then ensued some of the most trying years in the existence of the White Sox. The will of Lou Comiskey placed the club in trust for his son, Charles A. Comiskey II, until such time as the grandson of the founder of the dynasty came of age. The trustee was the First National Bank of Chicago, but the will specified that Grabiner, the faithful steward, should carry on as he had been doing through the declining years of Charles A. Comiskey as well as in Lou's time as sole owner of the club.

Surviving Lou Comiskey was his widow, Grace, two daughters, Dorothy and Gracie Lu, and the son, Charles A. II. The son was in his teens and pursuing his education. The two daughters were employees of the club, Dorothy holding a responsible position.

The financial entanglements of the White Sox, with a bank suddenly thrust into the baseball business, created a situation that was awkward, to say the least, and one that was resented greatly by Mrs. Comiskey, a high-spirited lady.

In Lou Comiskey's lifetime various responsible persons had made attempts to buy the White Sox, but each proposition had been rejected. Shortly before his death, Lou

Comiskey had entertained a project of moving to another part of Chicago from the site where the White Sox had functioned since 1910. This plan might have introduced capital other than that of the Comiskeys into the club for the first time, and it certainly would have meant a tremendous new ball park in a more desirable location. But Lou Comiskey's death intervened. In the period when the day-book and ledger brigade from the bank was in charge, those who had gained Lou Comiskey's attention now lost interest in the idea.

With the bank in charge, more attempts were made to purchase the White Sox. Some of them became so insistent, Mrs. Grace Comiskey moved to have the will broken that she might take over herself, with Grabiner's aid, and maintain all the family traditions until Charles II was ready to follow in the footsteps of his father and his grandfather.

In 1941, Mrs. Comiskey succeeded in regaining control of the property and became the head of the White Sox organization. In October of that same year, John D. Rigney married Dorothy Comiskey.

The official White Sox family party now included Mrs. Comiskey, president; two daughters, Dorothy Comiskey Rigney and Gracie Lu, treasurer and assistant secretary, respectively; Joe Barry, brother-in-law of Mrs. Comiskey, traveling secretary; and Rigney, son-in-law, a member of the pitching staff. Charles A. II, the son, had not made up his mind whether he would rather be a player with the White Sox or their president. He rather leaned to the first idea, just then.

Dykes, the voluble manager, succeeded in bringing the club home in third place for the 1941 season. This was the third time he had done that since taking over. Since the club finished exactly at the .500 mark, winning seventy-seven and losing seventy-seven, while the New York Yankees, the championship winners were twenty-one games in front, even Dykes did not make too much of the finish. However, fretful over his own fate of having to make a race with castoffs from other clubs and a rarely occasional minor-league find of his very own. Dykes about this time took off on the subject of Joe McCarthy, the very successful Yankee manager.

"Who couldn't be a success with that material?" Dykes demanded. "When he needs a player, all he has to do is push a button and one jumps in from Kansas City or Newark or somewhere else where the Yankees have them hidden out awaiting the call."

Dykes was to get more mileage out of this branding of McCarthy as a push-button manager than he ever drew from his frequent biting observations on American League umpires, rival ball players, and kindred subjects.

This 1941 third-place finish, it so happened, was to be the highest point reached by Dykes while directing the White Sox.

Complications of existence continued as the club worried along without adequate working capital. Its problems might have been more pronounced but for the fact that all other clubs and the world at large began to have troubles of their own, following the Japs' sneak attack at Pearl Harbor, December 7, 1941.

During the war years the White Sox did the best they could with what they had. One by one, component parts of the club, such as Ted Lyons, Bob Kennedy, John Rigney, Taft Wright, Don Kolloway, who had joined the team in 1941, and finally, Luke Appling, the man of no waste motion, entered the Armed Forces.

Play throughout the American League was at a low ebb because the wealth of talent was off to the wars. The Sox drifted back to sixth place in 1942, but climbed back to fourth the following season.

This was Appling's last before entering the Army, and

as a farewell he blasted out a .328 average that was good enough to lead the depleted American League hitters.

One of Dykes' rummage-sale players, outfielder Wally Moses, chose this 1943 season to be the one in which he stole fifty-six bases. That was high for the club's history, and remained a challenge even for Orestes Minoso, Jim Busby, and the other sprightly members of the "Go ChicaGO Sox!" who were to make 1951 baseball history. Regrettably Moses' performance at no time struck the responsive chord that did Appling's batting, and for a long time Comiskey Park missed the resounding cries of "Come on Luke!" that invariably accompanied each appearance of Appling at the plate.

When Dykes gained fourth place in 1943 it represented the sixth time in nine complete seasons he had made the first division. This was a praiseworthy record for since the expenditure of $150,000 for Al Simmons, Mule Haas, and himself there had been no extraordinary spending sprees on the part of the ownership to get him ball players. Few other major-league clubs were operated on that basis. The struggle of the Comiskeys against the wealth several clubs in their own league could marshal against them was at times desperate. However, the club proudly points to the fact that whether profits were sizable, small, or none at all, White Sox bills were all paid, in bad years as well as in good.

For more than forty years of the club's existence, the White Sox operated without the aid of "farm" clubs. Many of their rivals found these minor-league affiliations handy for the development and advancement of material. The White Sox had working agreements with few minor-league clubs. As late as 1938 the entire scouting system was so small that it was carried on the roster under the heading: "Scouts: Mr. and Mrs. Roy Largent."

It was common belief that the scouting system was made

up of an annual baseball guide's records, some stamps, stationery, and Harry Grabiner's unbounded faith that next year was really going to be the White Sox year if all of those players found in the minor-league batting, fielding, and pitching averages only looked half that good when Dykes got them into training camp.

Only one with access to all the information regarding the handicaps under which the organization was run can realize that it was not only amazing the White Sox did as well as they were doing, but somewhat surprising that they were able to exist at all. Over all hung that tragicomic suggestion, now akin to a tradition, that things happened to the White Sox that could happen only to them.

In one of the war years, for example, when a ruling of Commissioner Landis caused all major-league clubs to train in the North, the White Sox prepared to camp near French Lick Springs, Indiana, where the Chicago Cubs were installed. When the White Sox arrived they found the spring freshets had made their practice field impossible for baseball purposes.

Undismayed, manager Dykes merely asked the Cubs to move over, and the White Sox charged right in. They got through their training spell somehow, even as they had been getting through all else, year after year.

They were approaching in the late months of 1944 a series of occurrences that were to change the entire baseball picture.

On November 25, that year, Commissioner Landis died. His secretary and faithful coworker, Leslie M. O'Connor, held sway in the office until organized baseball chose a successor for the illustrious first commissioner. The choice was Senator Albert B. Chandler of Kentucky. For some months after he took office O'Connor remained with him. O'Connor was an expert on baseball law, its rules and regulations, and saw to it that every *i* was dotted and every *t* was crossed. Only Landis himself and a few close friends knew how important a part O'Connor had played since he was first chosen secretary by the man who lifted organized base-ball out of the chaos in which the old National Commissioner triumvirate had left it twenty-three years before.

There were many at the time of the death of Landis who believed that baseball would be well served if O'Connor were named his successor. There were some who thought O'Connor wanted the post. He did not. He had been browsing in baseball's bylaws and records long enough. He wanted to get out and look around. As soon as he felt that Chandler, the new commissioner, was adjusted to his surroundings, O'Connor resigned, he said, to take life easy.

Not long after this, the White Sox entered the Commissioner's picture. Herold (Muddy) Ruel, the same who had been readying the broken-down and the underripe pitchers for Jimmy Dykes, was, among other things, an able barrister. His baseball knowledge, coupled with his legal training, eminently fitted Ruel, in Chandler's judgment, for the position as aide to the Commissioner.

On November 3, 1945, Muddy Ruel undertook a career of getting Chandler's briefs in as good shape as he had been getting Dykes' pitchers. Did quite well at it, to, but not well enough nor happily enough to cause him to pass up a chance to manage the St. Louis Browns in 1947. All the while he had been with the White Sox Ruel's managerial potentialities had been the subject for discussion, but whether he could be a good manager or not is still debatable. The St. Louis Browns of 1947 vintage, on the field and in the front office, were such as to defy the managerial talents of the greatest manager who ever lived. After one season Ruel asked for and obtained commutation of his sentence. He was prepared to secure a writ of habeas corpus to get himself out if need be.

Only one other club in baseball was comparable with

the Browns for the complexities of its inner workings. That was the White Sox. Late in 1945, Harry Grabiner, who had been with it through all its ups and downs since 1905, bade farewell to Mrs. Grace Comiskey, wished all the luck in the world to her, to her daughters, her son, her son-in-law, and to her brothers-in-law (another of whom, Frank McMahon, had replaced Joe Barry as traveling secretary), and went forth, he said, to take life easy.

But Grabiner didn't mean it, any more than Les O'Connor had when he left Commissioner Chandler. Taking life easy just wasn't in the book for such as Harry Grabiner or Les O'Connor.

CHAPTER TWENTY-EIGHT

THE beginning of the end for Jimmy Dykes was in sight as the White Sox droned through the 1945 season, finishing in sixth place. Dykes, one of the foremost umpire baiters, was now showing visible signs of growing tired of it all. He weighed the possibilities of managing his listless squad without donning a uniform. The only other major-league manager to scorn his team's regalia was the venerable Connie Mack, until Burt Shotton came along as emergency leader of the Brooklyn Dodgers, but even Shotton made the concession of wearing his club's familiar blue cap.

Dykes had perfect understanding with Harry Grabiner and when the latter left the White Sox it was thought that a change in management was imminent. However, the situation with respect to a field leader remained unchanged during the winter. Not so the Department of the Interior. During the 1945 world's series which engaged the interest of the Detroit Tigers and Chicago Cubs, it became noised about that Les O'Connor, former associate of Commissioners Landis and Chandler, was to take up the burden laid down by Grabiner. The news, incidentally, broke before the White Sox were ready to announce it formally, but

O'Connor himself, present at the world's series, made no great attempt to side-step its confirmation.

O'Connor accepted the post as general manager only after an understanding with Mrs. Comiskey that some of the conditions which had made Grabiner's stay impossible would be rectified. Chief of these was his insistence that the Comiskey purse be loosened more often that the ball park and the ball club might be better fitted to proceed in a major-league manner.

The new general manager recognized, as did the fans of Chicago, that Comiskey Park's once beautiful face was in great need of an uplift. Grabiner had recognized it, too, but approached the matter with the wrong technique. On one occasion he wanted to purchase new chairs to replace those which had been in use since 1926, and some since 1910 when the park first opened. But Grabiner asked for the money first, and was frowned upon. O'Connor's plan was to have the work done first, have the bills submitted, and let it go at that. The bills were paid, that being an old White Sox custom, and only a few knew that the chairs O'Connor had installed at swollen post-war prices were the same Grabiner could have bought and certainly tried to buy at much less cost years before. But Grabiner had been told in effect that everything was going along all right as it was.

The park reconditioning was something the new general manager could attend to without delay. Reconditioning of the ball club was something else again. There was no immediate route to that objective. Trades with other major-league clubs, even for the sort of shopworn material which had been coming Dykes' way in previous years, were out of the question. The White Sox had nothing to offer that they could afford to let go from their own modest store of acceptable players. Other clubs were not interested in money even if O'Connor's technique was such that he could get the checks signed. There remained then the long haul, the roll-your-own development plan—in other words, a farm system. O'Connor busied himself with that, and the number of minor-league clubs which were welded into a White Sox chain grew with the passing days.

O'Connor's long years of silence while serving in the office of baseball's Commissioner had not fitted him for any energetic open display of his activities as general manager of the White Sox. He had not acquired the habit of personal projection. He worked long hours and was at all times available for inquiry. When a reporter asked questions, O'Connor answered them, but the news of the White Sox had to be of great importance for the general manager to volunteer any statements. For the first few months of his term in office reaction of press and public seemed to be that news of the White Sox could not possibly be of any interest to anyone but the White Sox themselves.

As O'Connor hewed to the line at Comiskey Park and kept his own counsel, Grabiner, the White Sox alumnus, was launching himself into a new career where he could explore all the modern angles of the principle of spending money to make money. This was the principle he had first seen invoked by Charles A. Comiskey, founder of the dynasty, but which had long since been abandoned by his successors.

To get the proper perspective on Grabiner's new activity it is necessary to go back to the days before World War II when the White Sox and the Cubs were steady patrons of the post-season baseball art known as the City Series. Grabiner, as the White Sox man in charge of such things, would undertake to check up box-office statements, ticket counts, gate receipts, and such items. In charge of the Cubs' end of such detail was young Bill Veeck, whose father contributed much to Cub baseball history as president of the club.

The younger Veeck came on the City Series scene equipped with adding machines, comptometers, and all other kinds of apparatus calculated to make the count come out accurately. Grabiner worked with a pencil and a pad of paper. It intrigued the young Veeck greatly that all his modern calculating equipment invariably came up with the same totals Grabiner had figured on his scratch pad with much less expenditure of time and patience pressing keys and pulling levers.

Veeck became a close friend of Grabiner's and often turned to the older and more experienced baseball man for advice even though they were associated with rival teams. All the while Veeck, who was to blossom forth one day as baseball's ranking promotional genius, was fretting at the conservative way things were going with the Cubs. He was a youth who had supreme confidence in himself and his undertakings, and while most of his ideas seemed radical to the Cubs, Veeck had faith in their workability. He kept on offering them to any who would listen, right on up to P. K. Wrigley, owner of the club. More often than not Wrigley wasn't having any, and eventually, as Veeck tells it, Wrigley would start shaking his head "No!" as he saw the youngster approach and without waiting to hear the latest proposition.

Early in June, 1941, Veeck decided to branch out for himself and he persuaded Charlie Grimm, then a coach with the Cubs, to enter into a proposition with him whereby they would take over the Milwaukee club. As owner, with Grimm a perfect foil for all of his eccentric operations, Veeck launched into an administration that very soon had the American Association and most of the rest of organized baseball marveling at the success of his methods.

The partnership had fun galore and made money at Milwaukee. Grimm eventually chose to return to the Cubs as their manager and Veeck carried on alone, either in person or by very remote control from the islands in the Pacific whence he had been dispatched as a member of the United States Marine Corps. Three pennants in a row through 1943, 1944, and 1945 came Milwaukee's way, along with attendance records up and down the American Association circuit as the fans endorsed to the utmost the Veeck methods of putting on a baseball show.

In March, 1944, on Bougainville, the faulty recoil of a 90-millimeter gun he was firing resulted in injury to Veeck's right leg which eventually necessitated amputation. A long siege of hospitalization followed. Veeck was released from one of these hospitals in time to see his club play its final game in 1945. He was not certain then of his physical future and when the chance presented itself, he sold the Milwaukee property. He intended to retire, he said, to Tucson, Arizona, and spend the rest of his life watching the cactus grow.

In the spring of 1946 when the White Sox and Cubs came through Arizona on their spring exhibition tour Veeck said he had made an important discovery about cactus. It did not grow more than an inch a year. Watching it grow was not nearly as exciting as he had thought it would be. When the ball clubs left Arizona on their way East, Veeck left with them. Presently he sought out his old friend, Harry Grabiner, who was discovering that life could be very boresome out of baseball for anyone who had spent forty years in it.

Veeck had made up his mind to get back into baseball. This time he wanted to own and operate a major-league franchise. As a Chicagoan, his first thought was of acquiring the White Sox. He had every reason to believe that P. K. Wrigley would not sell the Cubs, or if he ever did, would not sell them to Bill Veeck. He was certain that the White Sox franchise was a property with which he might do even greater deeds than had been wrought at Milwaukee. As one who had spent so many years with the White Sox, Grabiner fitted into Veeck's plans for the approach on the Comiskeys. The project did not get as far as a bidding stage, for the Comiskeys were firm in their refusal to sell either in part or the entire franchise.

Now that they were committed to a return to baseball, Veeck and Grabiner did not abandon the search. They sounded out possibilities in several major-league cities and came at last to Cleveland, where their sales talk met with success. It was not a deal which could be swung overnight. The combined capital of Veeck and Grabiner was not sufficient, and both were busy rounding up interested parties. It was Grabiner's persuasive eloquence that was responsible for much of the Chicago money which figured in the transfer of the Cleveland franchise to Veeck, and when the deal was finally closed, the former White Sox general manager moved into Cleveland as one of the executives. He was supremely content now. He was associated with the one man who was willing to cater to Grabiner's long-suppressed desire to exploit the theory of making money in baseball by spending money.

Veeck's operations with the Cleveland club make up baseball's most spectacular story of success, artistically and financially. Many of his sideshow entertainments nettled baseball's reactionaries, but for all of his flair for fun and frolic at Cleveland as at Milwaukee, Veeck never once lost sight of the axiom that there is no substitute for a winning baseball club.

In his own way and in his own time, which was as quickly as it could possibly be done, Veeck assembled not only an American League pennant winner but a world's championship club, the first Cleveland had owned in twenty-eight years. Along the way all of baseball's attendance records were smashed as Veeck's methods caught the popular fancy.

The reaction to all this in Chicago where Veeck had

grown up and gained his early knowledge of baseball was most pronounced. In the season the Cleveland Indians surged to a world's championship, both White Sox and Cubs settled into last place in their respective leagues. Cub followers regretted greatly that the imaginative Veeck had been permitted to get away. The knowledge that he had tried and failed to acquire the White Sox before going to Cleveland left a feeling of regret with many of the Comiskey Park addicts who had been yearning for years for some excitement. They bemoaned the fact that their experience with the Veeck methods were restricted to the eleven occasions on which the Indians came to Comiskey Park annually.

What the sentiment of the Comiskeys themselves was to all this stir was not disclosed. However, when they counted the receipts at the end of any White Sox vs. Indians series, at Comiskey Park or at Cleveland, they were probably very grateful that they did get to see a Veeck project twenty-two times a season.

Indirectly the White Sox were involved in one of the more spectacular of Veeck's bids for attention—the signing of the fabulous Negro pitcher, Satchel Paige. There had been some discussion as to whether Paige's entry into the ranks of the Indians had been motivated as much by his potential pitching skill as by his crowd-gathering appeal.

On the night of August 13, 1948, with proper advance notice, of course, Satchel Paige was sent against the White Sox in the presence of 51,599 at Comiskey Park. He turned in a shutout victory, one of his several pitching exploits which were to prove that the ancient Paige could still fool batsmen as well as divert record crowds which had come out to see him. This 51,599 attendance mark was to stand as a single game record for Comiskey Park until the high flying Sox of 1951 played a night game with the New York Yankees with 53,940 in the stands.

The tumult and the shouting which accompanied Veeck's rise to master of all he surveyed in baseball was not heard by his old friend, Grabiner. He was confined to his Chicago home by illness when the Indians crashed through in 1948 against the Boston Braves. He died a few weeks later, and his passing was mourned greatly by all who had known and respected him for his tireless efforts in baseball, forty years of it in the service of the White Sox.

CHAPTER TWENTY-NINE

NOTHING that Les O'Connor was able to do during the months preceding the 1946 season was calculated to improve the White Sox standing on the playing field and no one had expected that it would. Not the least of those who failed to be impressed by the outlook was Jimmy Dykes. On May 25, lacking sixteen days of having managed the club for an even dozen years, he offered his resignation, which was accepted. One of Dykes' several claims to distinction in the story of the White Sox was the duration of his managerial sway. None of the sixteen who had tried it before him was willing to stick to it out for anywhere near that length of time.

The White Sox did not have to look very far for a successor to Dykes. They hit upon Ted Lyons, the pitcher, who had been with the club continuously since 1923 save for the war years which he spent with the Marines. Lyons was regarded as a logical choice by all who gave a passing thought to the downtrodden White Sox. He did not, however, leap at the offer to manage the club when it was first tendered him. Lyons was a most intelligent sort who had served the White Sox through several managerial orders and no one knew any better than he did that the best he might get would be the worst of it, once he was placed in control of the players. His loyalty to the club as much as anything else moved him to give it a try at least for the balance of the 1946 season. When his acceptance was announced the selection was hailed with delight by Chicagoans generally.

In making Lyons No. 18 in the series of managers, the Comiskeys were adopting the policy the founder of the dynasty had followed long years before. Charles A. Comiskey had given to Jimmy Callahan, Fielder Jones, Billy Sullivan, Eddie Collins, and Ray Schalk the chance to try their hand at managing the club to which they had given many or all of their playing years.

It happened that Lyons was the first pitcher to get the managerial chance at the White Sox since Clark Griffith handled the club in 1901. Other stalwart White Sox pitchers such as Big Ed Walsh and Red Faber had been assigned coaching jobs, and while Callahan had begun his baseball career as a pitcher, he had turned to the outfield when the first Comiskey tapped him on the shoulder and said "take charge."

Lyons did not have to be a very close student of baseball history to know that if he were able to work a latter-day miracle and do something startling with the White Sox he would be the first pitcher since Griffith to make a success of running a major-league club. Many others had tried it in both the American and National leagues. None had succeeded, though in their number were listed the pitching immortals, Christy Mathewson and Walter Johnson, and such fiery competitors as Wild Bill Donovan and Burleigh Grimes. Pitchers just did not seem to be proper managerial material, but the White Sox liked Lyons and Lyons, who had never worked for any other organization, liked the White Sox. He picked up the pieces left on the board by the departing Jimmy Dykes and was pleasantly surprised when the club finished in fifth place, missing a .500 rating for the season by six points.

The managerial change, some of Les O'Connor's efforts to dress up the park, and general interest reflected in baseball throughout the country helped the White Sox attract 983,403 through their gates for the 1946 season. This exceeded by 149,911 the greatest previous seasonal attendance in White Sox history. The record that was broken had belonged to the White Sox of 1920. In that year 833,492 had come out to see in action the very players who were then being subjected to the scrunity of owner Comiskey and all his investigators, as the attempt was being made to find out just what had happened in the 1919 world's series of unhappy memory.

Reaction to this fine artistic and financial flourish after all the lean years was such that the White Sox and their following now actually looked forward to the 1947 season with some interest rather than the dread which had been an annual incident in so many of the previous years.

The Department of the Interior now presented a solid wall of the Comiskey clan, broken only by the presence of general manager Les O'Connor. It included Mrs. Grace Comiskey, president; Mrs. Dorothy Comiskey Rigney, treasurer; Grace Lu Comiskey, assistant secretary; and Frank McMahon, traveling secretary. John D. Rigney had put aside his pitching career to become director of the farm clubs which O'Connor was steadily rounding up so that the White Sox might one day roll their own.

The growth of the farm system had called for a great increase in the number of scouts. In this group were listed Patsy O'Rourke, Fred Lear, Joseph O'Rourke, William Buckley, Douglas Minor, Maurice Robinson, Charles Sanhuber, George Seneker, Leonard Tree, Emmett Ormsby, Paul Neil, Ellsworth Brown, Frank Bridges, Hal Trosky, Irvine F. Jeffries, and John Kerr. Ormsby was the former American League umpire who had retired after long service. Trosky was a first baseman who had come to the White Sox from Cleveland, and held forth for several seasons. Kerr was also a former White Sox infielder. Sixteen good men and true, beating the bushes throughout the country in quest of material that might be had for the White Sox—if the price were not too high.

A far cry, indeed, from the recruiting system which had been in vogue when the club's line on prospects was no more personal than the survey of a few lines of facts and figures in an annual baseball guide. In reality, however, the White Sox scouting squad was a rather modest array by contrast with those in the employ of other major-league clubs, nor were any of them so well paid that they could devote all their time to the quest for baseball material.

Across town where the rival Cubs operated, Jack Sheehan, farm director, had at his command forty-three scouts. Two of them, interestingly enough, were Ray Schalk and Mervyn Shea, both of whom had playing records with the White Sox. Schalk, of course, was the White Sox No. 1 catcher in the club's all-time rating.

In this presentation of the 1947 line-up and batting order of the Comiskey family, blood or marital relatives, the name of Charles A. II for whom the property was held in trust does not appear. He had no title just then. He was completing his formal education but appeared periodically in White Sox affairs, a rather precocious youth. He had given up the idea that he might be one of the players. Now he was waiting impatiently for the time when he could step into the organization, take full charge and perhaps straighten out everything.

He was heard once from a seat in the White Sox dugout during a game at Comiskey Park. He had no right to be there, but the offense against baseball rules might have been overlooked if he had not attempted to emulate Jimmy

Dykes and express himself forcibly and with gestures when a decision went against the White Sox. President Will Harridge's umpires have a normal sense of humor and are willing to go along with a gag as well as anyone. But young Comiskey's performance was definitely out of bounds. He was guilty of disturbing the peace and quiet which the umpires had accepted as a natural consequence of the ennui which had gripped the White Sox. That was unforgivable.

Charles A. Comiskey II was given the bum's rush out of the dugout. He was told to get the hell off that bench and stay off. The chastened owner-to-be beat an undignified retreat and the incident was given adequate treatment in the Chicago papers. Many who had forgotten there was a Charles A. Comiskey II began to take notice. It was a fine start for a young man who might then have been plotting a career as an exhibitionist, but he did not have a follow through.

After this brief bid for attention not much more was heard of the young man until late in 1947. In the interval the White Sox, after their sudden flare-up, returned to the smoldering state. No one did much that was exciting. Nobody seemed to worry too much that it wasn't exciting. Attendance held up remarkably well, for there were some great clubs in the American League and when they came to Comiskey Park there were sizable turnouts of fans to greet them. The installation of lights, projected in Lou Comiskey's time and completed after his death, helped materially in the attendance, but the club remained anchored securely in the second division.

Night baseball in Chicago was possible only at Comiskey Park, for P. K. Wrigley, owner of the Cubs, steadfastly refused to erect light towers at the field which bore his family name. Nor could anyone take him to task for insisting that baseball was a day game. Year after year, no matter whether the Cubs were a pennant contender or back among the also rans, Wrigley Field played to astonishing attendance figures. They exceeded the Comiskey Park totals season after season, right along, even though the years 1946 with their record total, and 1947 with the second highest figure of 876,948 were written into the White Sox annals. In this stretch the Cubs were far off the pennant race, as were the White Sox, so there really wasn't any accounting for Chicago's baseball tastes.

As the White Sox moved unmajestically through the 1947 season, one of the club's scouts was studying the actions of a Chicago prep-school pitcher. In time he notified general manager O'Connor that here was a prospect who looked so good he merited a bonus for signing a contract. He could mean much to the future of the White Sox, the scout insisted. No scout in all history, starting with those J. Fenimore Cooper first extolled, ever spoke truer words. This young prep-school pitcher was to cause an upheaval that was to be felt around the entire baseball world. It was in perfect accord with the tradition that things happened to the White Sox which could happen only to them. This one, however, topped 'em all. Comes now the revolution!

CHAPTER THIRTY

On the twenty-ninth of October, general manager Les O'Connor of the White Sox issued a brief statement to the press. For refusing to pay a $500 fine assessed against the White Sox for signing pitcher George Zoeterman in attendance at Chicago Christian High School, the club had been suspended by Commissioner A. B. Chandler from all the rights and benefits under the major-league rules, O'Connor said. Zoeterman had been summarily declared a free agent by the Commissioner, and upon completion of his high-school course would be open for propositions from any club except the White Sox.

The impact of this brief statement was terrific. The White Sox, whose original owner had helped found the American League, were now out of the baseball business. Nothing like that had ever happened before in the entire history of the league.

Phones, local and long distance, were commandeered by batteries of Chicago news gatherers. Commissioner Chandler at Cincinnati was not immediately available. He had issued no statement with regard to any situation between the White Sox and the Commissioner's office, and until O'Connor's statement was released no one suspected that there had been a brush between Chandler and the man who for so many years had interpreted the rules and prepared the briefs in the administration of Judge Landis.

O'Connor's stand was that the rule which Chandler said had been violated did not cover Zoeterman's case. The White Sox, he said, were prepared to fight this one to a finish. They would take it if necessary into civil court, even though organized baseball had always shunned the civil courts as a place to settle any of its arguments. O'Connor, having delivered his original stirring statement, refused to amplify it.

Lacking any immediate word from Chandler, the eager reporters aimed their questions at Will Harridge, the president of the American League. Did this decision of the Commissioner mean that the league now had but seven clubs? It did. Did it mean that with the draft and other American and interleague meetings coming up the White Sox would not be allowed to participate, even by proxy? It did. Did it mean that the 1948 schedule would have to be drawn up to include seven clubs if the unprecedented situation were not cleared up in the meanwhile? It did.

Harridge, a fighter when he had to be, but normally a peace loving man, was hopeful that O'Connor and Chandler would see eye to eye before all these possible eventualities came to pass. But he was given scant encouragement by O'Connor who was bristling with indignation and prepared to fight the case to a finish. He had the backing of the ball club. Or so he thought. His rebellion against Chandler had taken place only after the Comiskeys had weighed the possibilities of the revolt.

A survey of the baseball code disclosed that at their joint meeting in New York, February 2, 1946, the major leagues had passed a rule prohibiting clubs from signing any student of a high school which is a member of the National Federation of State Athletic Associations.

In subsequent bulletins from his office Chandler had indicated that he intended to regard this rule as covering all high-school players. This, then, was the point at issue. O'Connor presumably refused to accept the Commissioner's power to interpret a rule except in the letter of the law passed by the leagues in joint session. He contended that the high school Zoeterman attended did not belong to any Federation. It did not even have a team of its own, and Zoeterman's pitching activity was confined to outside teams. He pitched for no American Legion team, whose membership is also protected from professional baseball raids. Therefore, Zoeterman's case was not covered by any rule in the book, O'Connor's legal mind argued.

O'Connor was certain that the White Sox were within their rights when they signed Zoeterman, after having first given him a bonus payment. No baseball rule was violated, or at least none that O'Connor had ever read was violated. Those who were aware of his familiarity with baseball law were inclined to make the snap judgment that if O'Connor hadn't heard of the law, then the law simply didn't exist.

The fact remained that Chandler was baseball's boss. He had decreed there was a violation of the rules. He had assessed the $500 fine. He had notified O'Connor of the "or else" alternative. O'Connor had chosen the "or else" by refusing to pay the fine. The White Sox were out of baseball until the fine was paid.

When neither side showed any signs of weakening, President Harridge of the American League was forced to call an emergency meeting in Cleveland to discuss the situation. O'Connor was the league's representative on baseball's executive council. If he as well as the White Sox chose to remain in outer darkness, a new executive council member had to be chosen. Ben Fiery, attorney for the league and secretary of the Cleveland Indians, took over the job while O'Connor's status was in doubt.

O'Connor arrived at the Cleveland meeting still in a warlike mood as newspapermen from all parts of the major-league territory crowded around. Those normally interested in baseball were joined by the considerable delegation on hand to cover the Notre Dame-Navy football game being played in Cleveland that week end.

After all this build-up for a battle to the finish, O'Connor and the newsmen present were all dismayed when a press association carried a dispatch from Minneapolis. There the irrepressible Charles A. Comiskey II had stepped out of his character as a college student long enough to announce that the $500 fine was going to be paid. In that case the shooting war was all over, with O'Connor not getting near enough to Chandler to see the whites of his eyes.

Here was a hastily convened meeting in Cleveland, called to discuss affairs of paramount importance to Chicago and the rest of the American League. And there was young Comiskey calmly announcing in Minneapolis what representatives of his own town's papers as well as those from all other major-league cities had expended both time and money to come to Cleveland to find out. Something like that could be done only by the White Sox.

There were no repercussions of the Zoeterman case after the fine was paid and the young player made a free agent. In due time he completed his high-school studies and listened to all propositions made by all the major-league scouts. He accepted an offer from the Chicago Cubs. He was dispatched to one of their farm clubs, presently to be lost sight of completely.

White Sox general manager O'Connor, close mouthed as ever, had no statement to make about the surprising rebuff young Comiskey's action had given him. However, it was plain that he accepted the fact that he was on the outside looking in when it came to serious operations involving the Comiskey dynasty.

The club's rights to participate in major-league affairs were restored with the paying of the fine. Actually the club had been out of baseball for the period from October 24 to November 4.

Because the Zoeterman case presented a situation in White Sox affairs akin to the Jack Quinn affair of 1918, a brief from Commissioner Chandler's office is presented. It sets forth, step by step, his original decision and a summary of all the facts in the case. It serves to show how far baseball had progressed in the orderly administration of its affairs since 1918. To appreciate completely that this is so, the suggestion is made that the reader, after absorbing the "play by play" of Chandler's report, return to the somewhat unintelligible specimen of the 1918 National Commission's attempt to clarify its findings in the case of Jack Quinn.

It should be remembered that there was no intimation whatever by Commissioner Chandler that an awkward situation had arisen between him and O'Connor until the latter broke the story with his own statement in Chicago. As a matter of fact the Commissioner, until his hand was forced, showed no sign of getting tough about it. Quite the contrary. His decision, assessing the fine and declaring the player a free agent, was issued September 26, 1947. The concluding paragraph set forth that the payment of the fine was to be made within *ten* days from the date.

Yet it was not until October 24 that Commissioner Chandler reminded O'Connor that the fine had not been paid. Things began to happen rapidly after that.

The original decision of Chandler, given September 26 and addressed to all major- and minor-league clubs, reads as follows:

The Chicago American League Club has signed player George G. Zoeterman to a professional baseball contract for the balance of the 1947 season as "batting practice pitcher," and to a regular player's contract for the season of 1948. Zoeterman is a student at the Chicago Christian High School, a parochial school which is not a member of the National Federation of State High School Athletic Associations. He will not graduate until January, 1948.

While Major-Minor League Rule 3 (1) specifies that "No student of a high school which is a member of the National Federation of State High School Athletic Associations shall be signed to a professional baseball contract until the day following his graduation, etc.," the rule has uniformly been interpreted as covering all high school students in the United States and Canada. Bulletins from this office were issued March 4, 1946, and February 7, 1947, in which this fact is made very clear. The Commissioner's office could not administer the rule in any other fashion, and the Commissioner has no intention of attempting to do so. Students could be withdrawn from high schools that are members of the Federation and entered into parochial schools that are not members, thereby evading the rule.

I am advised that no parochial school in the Chicago City League is a member, while parochial schools in the remainder of Illinois are members.

One of the provisions of the High School Rule is that "any contract made in violation shall be declared null and void, and the offending club shall be permanently prohibited from using such player." Another provision of the rule is that the offending club shall be fined $500.

Clearly, the Chicago American League Club has violated the spirit of the High School Rule in signing Zoeterman. Both the contracts between Zoeterman and the Chicago American League Club are declared void, and the club or any affiliate thereof is permanently prohibited from signing George G. Zoeterman to a professional baseball contract.

Two current White Sox stars, Orestes Minoso, infielder-outfielder, and
Chico Carrasquel. (*Chicago Herald American Photo.*)

Two White Sox managers meet with the front office. General Manager Frank Lane, Charles A. Comiskey II, and Jack Onslow, manager, 1949-1950. (*Chicago Herald American Photo*.)

The current White Sox manager, Paul Richards, signing his contract in 1951 with Lane and Comiskey looking on. (*Chicago Herald American Photo*.)

The Chicago American League Club, moreover, is hereby fined the sum of $500, payment to be made to the Secretary-Treasurer of BASEBALL within ten days from this date.

O'Connor's contention was that he was not violating any law passed by the major leagues in joint session. He refused to accept the Commissioner's interpretation that the rule covered *all* high-school players, regardless of Federation affiliations. O'Connor was further willing to make something of the baseball legal point that Zoeterman's high school did not have a baseball team of its own, and therefore Federations or non-Federations did not concern it or Zoeterman.

To present factually what the shooting was all about and to trace the various steps which led to baseball's most unusual situation, there is a brief issued by Walter W. Mulbry, Secretary-Treasurer of BASEBALL, by direction of the Commissioner. Dated October 30, the day after O'Connor had broken the story of his revolt, it reads:

In order to clarify the situation surrounding the signing of player George G. Zoeterman to a professional baseball contract by the Chicago American League Club in violation of the High School Rule, the following facts are set forth:

On February 2, 1946, the Major Leagues at their Joint Meeting in New York passed the High School Rule, known as 3 (1). The rule became effective on March 4, 1946, the date on which the President of the National Association of Professional Baseball Leagues advised the Commissioner that the Association had approved the rule.

On that day a bulletin was issued by the Commissioner's office, quoting the rule and adding:

"The rule is the result of the intent and purpose of the Major Leagues and Minor Leagues to protect the eligibility of students attending any high school which is a member of the National Federation and of any student who has been eligible to such high school and whose class has not yet graduated. *However, please be advised that the Commissioner holds that the Major League Rule 3(1) and the Major-Minor League Rule 3(1) will be construed to include all high schools."*

Another bulletin was issued on February 7, 1947, which closed with the following paragraph:

"For the purpose of clarifying the rule, the following interpretations are set forth: (a) The rule is construed to include all high schools in the United States and Canada; (b) The day on which a boy's class receives diplomas will be considered the date of graduation."

No complaint had been received in this office from any club owners with respect to the Commissioner's interpretation of the rule until Mr. Leslie M. O'Connor, Vice President and General Manager of the Chicago American League Club, communicated with the Commissioner on August 2, 1947, saying:

"We have a request for a tryout from a boy who is attending a parochial high school. This high school does not have any baseball team and he is not connected with American Legion baseball in any way. We would like to know whether it is permissible to give him a tryout and sign him up if we think he has a chance in professional baseball."

Mr. O'Connor was informed, on August 5, that:

"If the boy in whom you are interested is a student in a parochial school he would be precluded from signing a baseball contract whether the school had a baseball team or not. The fact that he is a high school student would bar him."

Mr. O'Connor wrote again on August 7 and September 6, when he said in conclusion:

"I am regretfully obliged to inform you that I must and will, on behalf of this club, deal as I see fit with such players (meaning those who are students of schools not members of the Federation)."

The Commissioner replied to that letter:

"The High School Rule will continue to be enforced as I have explained it to you before."

On September 18, Mr. O'Connor advised the Commissioner that the Chicago American League Club had signed George Zoeterman to a baseball contract for 1948, and also as a batting practice pitcher for the remainder of this season.

The action constituted a direct defiance of the Commissioner's ruling.

On September 26, George Zoeterman was declared a free agent by the Commissioner and the Chicago club was fined $500 and precluded from ever re-signing Zoeterman. The Chicago club was directed to pay the fine within ten days.

The fine was not paid by October 24, and Commissioner Chandler advised Mr. O'Connor by teletype:

"In connection with the signing of George Zoeterman, I find that you have not complied with my directive of September 26 with respect to payment of five hundred dollar fine. Please do so promptly."

Mr. O'Connor replied:

"Your directive is in all respects illegal and we have no intention of paying fine or recognizing your right to void this entirely legal contract."

Commissioner Chandler thereupon sent the following teletype message:

"The Commissioner suspends as of October 24, 1947, the benefits of all Major League Rules to the Chicago American League Club until his directive of September 26 is complied with, and deprives the Chicago American League Club and its General Manager, Leslie M. O'Connor, from representation at any and all meetings under the Major League agreement until further notice."

No advice of the Commissioner's action was released to the Press from this office until Mr. O'Connor announced in Chicago, on October 29, that he had been "suspended" by Commissioner Chandler.

Such things could happen only to the White Sox.

CHAPTER THIRTY-ONE

IF the White Sox supplied excitement for those few days of the off season, they were not to create more than mild diversion once the clubs began training for 1948. This was to be a year in which the American League presented a race that eclipsed all previous pennant quests for sheer baseball drama. It involved four clubs most of the way, before the Cleveland Indians finally defeated the last challenger, the Boston Red Sox. To do that a post-season game was required, since the two had completed the regular 154 game schedule in an exact tie. The New York Yankees were not shaken off until two days before the season's close, and the fourth legitimate contender, the Philadelphia Athletics, remained in the race until a few weeks before that.

The White Sox unfortunately were destined to finish in last place, losing 101 games.

Cleveland won the one game play-off from Boston and went on to gain the world's championship from the Boston Braves in a six-game series that found all-time series attendance records falling by the wayside as Bill Veeck's tremendous following surged into the Cleveland Stadium for the three games played there.

Reflected glory on the field and at the box office was all

the White Sox had in this memorable American League race, though two of their former players and one former coach were aligned with the Indians and shared in the world's series returns. One of the players was outfielder Thurman Tucker, whose principal claim to fame was his resemblance to Joe E. Brown of motion-picture, stage, and radio fame. He was one of the minor Cleveland defensive characters in the series. Another White Sox alumnus was Bob Kennedy who made the final put-out of the series. He had come to Cleveland in midseason in a trade for Pat Seerey, a burly outfielder on whom the Indians had expended the efforts of such notable experts as Rogers Hornsby and Tris Speaker in an attempt to turn Seerey's potential power into a steadily useful property. When he landed on a baseball Seerey was able to hit it as far as any-one of his time, but he had the unfortunate faculty of setting the strike-out record for the American League in many of his seasons.

All the skilled instruction from Speaker and Hornsby was not enough to balance Seerey's batting budget and it was with no regret that Bill Veeck agreed to his transfer to the White Sox. Nor did Veeck express any regret when the news reached him on July 18 that Seerey that day had slugged a bevy of Connie Mack's pitchers for four home runs in a game at Shibe Park, thereby getting himself into a class with such as Bobby Lowe, Ed Delehanty, Lou Gehrig, Chuck Klein, and Gil Hodges.

"Sure, Pat can hit a ball a mile when he hits it," sighed Veeck, when asked about this. "But how long can you wait?"

The nature of the American League race was such that attendance held up remarkably well all over the circuit. The White Sox participated in an attendance share far beyond what their own brand of baseball figured to attract. In one series, however, they threw a real block in Cleveland's progress by winning three games in a row when the

Indians had already counted them as their very own. The setback was but temporary, for Cleveland's brilliant force-of-example manager, Lou Boudreau, dragged them back from that misadventure and they went on to win, even though overtime was required.

The White Sox shared by remote control in the development of Cleveland pitching, particularly that of Gene Bearden, a newcomer. His great success in the critical stages of the race and in the world's series was traced to the teachings of Muddy Ruel. Ruel had joined the Indians as a coach following the escape from St. Louis where he had his fill of attempting to manage that kind of a club. Ruel had proven his worth as a coach of pitchers in the long years he had served with Jimmy Dykes at Comiskey Park, but none of his White Sox pupils ever responded to instruction as did Bearden, the young pitching sensation of 1948.

The rooting interest the White Sox and their following had in the doings of Ruel, Kennedy, and Tucker at Cleveland and the maintenance of a worth-while attendance were about all that 1948 offered for Chicago's American League representatives. The year brought with it more unrest than had been noticeable, even in the collapse of the Jimmy Dykes regime when no one seemed to care what happened or to whom it happened. There were continuous indications that another shake-up was in the making.

First intimation of this came during spring training after an exhibition game at San Francisco in which the White Sox were rudely treated by the Pacific Coast League club. Charles A. Comiskey II, along as an observer, was outspoken about the lackluster showing of his club. He expressed himself forcibly that matters had gone far enough and that something would have to be done about it. He wasn't quite sure just what. This was not surprising since his father and grandfather before him had held to much the same opinion since 1920, and nothing they could do seemed to rectify matters for long. However, Charles A. II broke into print with a bang. His utterances made much better copy than the daily recital of the failure of the players on the field.

On this same spring jaunt, traveling secretary Frank McMahon, in charge of what John Hoffman, a Chicago sports writer, termed the Department of Utter Confusion, brought the squad into Phoenix, Arizona, for a brief exhibition stay. It had been arranged for the club to stay at a tourist camp which was the base of operations for the New York Giants who trained at Phoenix. The Giants were away on an exhibition junket of their own, or so secretary McMahon had been led to believe. After considerable scrambling around he had succeeded in getting his party transported to the tourist camp and comfortably settled when the Giants suddenly returned to take over the borrowed quarters. Veteran members of the White Sox party did not lift an eyebrow at this. They were used to travel and transportation incidents which would have utterly dismayed a less hardy group.

There had been that time when the White Sox rushed from the St. Louis ball park following a night game to catch a train for Chicago. As is the custom, all hand luggage had been sent from the hotel directly to the railroad station as the party left for the ball park to fill its engagement. Only in this instance the Department of Utter Confusion had dispatched the luggage to one railroad station while the train on which the party was to travel left from an entirely different one.

All things considered, it is not surprising that the White Sox, taking off in all directions at once, did not make any progress in the forty-eighth year of their existence. That they finished in last place after having been there from opening day on surprised no one. But in so doing they managed to add a little touch here and there to make the performance distinctive. This time they lost 101 games, which were more than any other White Sox team except Fonseca's

Follies of 1932 had been able to do. They chose to get into last place again in the same year in which the Chicago Cubs were touching bottom in the National League, turning in the worst won and lost record in that club's history. A remarkable seasonal attendance of 777,844 in this sorry year testified that somebody still loved the White Sox, but it is doubtful if any of the Comiskeys were in that category. They could hardly wait for the season's end to get organized on a complete turnover of executives and playing personnel.

The first to go was Ted Lyons, who thus broke with the club with which he had been so completely identified in all his major-league career. A short time afterward, Jack Onslow, who had been managing the Memphis club, a White Sox affiliate, was named for the job. With him—though none suspected it at the time—was to begin an era in which White Sox doings were to reach a new high for attention in press, radio, and the latest medium of portrayal of fact and fancy, television.

Three seasons had now been completed under the general management of Les O'Connor. The White Sox established their all-time high attendance mark in his first year, set up their second highest in the next, and even in the third, or year of their dismantling, their attendance figures had been topped in but four other years of White Sox existence.

Coincident with the play-off game between Cleveland and Boston following the regular season's close, it was revealed in a Chicago newspaper that O'Connor several weeks before had tendered his resignation to take effect as soon as the Department of the Interior could refashion itself.

O'Connor, present at the Cleveland-Boston game, maintained his natural gift for issuing no statements. Any announcement of White Sox affairs he preferred to have made by the White Sox, he admitted to reporters who sought him out when the story first broke. The story also included the fact that Frank Lane, then president of the American Association, was to be the White Sox new general manager. Onslow, the new manager, was in Boston with O'Connor at the time the news of the change in general management broke into print.

In Chicago, Charles A. Comiskey II, acting as spokesman for the club, issued a general denial that O'Connor was out and Lane was in. Lane, winding up his affairs with the American Association, did some skilled side-stepping of pointed inquiries, all of which had no more effect than to irritate the forthright O'Connor who not only had resigned but had helped in the process of securing Lane to replace him.

Long before the world's series finished its two-game stand in Boston and turned toward Cleveland for the next three, it was generally accepted that the change in White Sox general management was as the newspaper stories indicated. Official confirmation from the Comiskeys was still lacking, however. That was being saved apparently for another day. When Charles II issued a call for a press conference after one of the series games at Cleveland and made the announcement that O'Connor had resigned and Lane was the new general manager, the news created almost as much excitement in Chicago as a report on the weather of the day before.

It was surmised that O'Connor's resignation had been brought about by continuing differences of opinion between himself and the ownership of the White Sox. He had effected many changes which removed much of the dry rot that had settled over Comiskey Park. He had ill luck in his quest for artistry on the ball field, though that was certainly nothing new in White Sox history since 1920.

It was suspected by many that his quashed rebellion against Commissioner Chandler was a contributing factor to O'Connor's retirement. Probably he did feel keenly the sudden change of mind on the part of the ownership after

196

he had committed himself to a battle to the finsh in the Zoeterman case. But he had been in baseball and through baseball's wars for a matter of twenty-eight years and he was intelligent enough a warrior to know when he was licked and a good enough sport to admit it.

In the department of sportsmanship Commissioner Chandler also qualified as an aftermath of the Zoeterman case. Concurrently with the major-league meetings in Chicago a few weeks after O'Connor had moved out of Comiskey Park, Chandler was host at a dinner to the club owners of the American and National leagues and to the leagues' executive staffs, as was his annual custom. At that dinner O'Connor was presented with a diamond studded watch as a memento of his twenty-eight years of service in the game. The watch was presented by Will Harridge, American League president, but it was the gift of Commissioner Chandler, BASEBALL, himself.

And none present on this happy occasion bothered to wonder whatever had become of George Zoeterman.

CHAPTER THIRTY-TWO

OVER the fireplace in the Bards Room at Comiskey Park there should hang one of the old copybook maxims, "If at first you don't succeed, try, try again."

That's what the White Sox of 1949 were doing, with an executive staff the like of which the club had never known before.

From the youthful owner, Charles Comiskey II, through general manager Frank Lane, field manager Jack Onslow, farm director John Rigney and his aide-de-camp, George Toporcer, right on down the line to the lowliest operative in the farm system, the trial and error process was invoked. There were mistakes. But the same mistakes were not made twice. The mistakes were not made without a prompt check being taken to find out who was responsible.

For a complete understanding of this new order of things at Comiskey Park it is fitting to study at length the careers and the personalities of Lane and Onslow who, within a year of their respective appointments, were to have the entire American League talking about them, as they were to talk of each other, very little of it complimentary.

How did it happen that Onslow had spent the last two thirds of his life—roughly two score years—in professional baseball without having his major-league managerial possibilities considered until he was approaching sixty?

"You can't answer that," said Onslow, "because it isn't strictly true. I was actually headed for a major-league managing job in the thirties when William Baker signed me as coach of the Phillies. Burt Shotton was then the manager. Baker said he wanted me to coach a year to get the hang of things and take over in 1932. Before my coaching term was up, Baker died. While I stayed on another season as coach I guess the managing job wasn't mentioned in his will."

Onslow regarded that as but one of three tough breaks that have been his since he began professional baseball as a catcher for Dallas in 1909. In the period from 1941 to 1947 he could not get any kind of a job in baseball. He had a series of severe illnesses in his family and he was desperate. But he couldn't get work as a coach, a scout, or as a manager. Boston baseball writers are credited by Onslow— a New England resident—with having kept him going by throwing occasional speaking engagements his way.

In order to emphasize what he considers the unkindest rap of all in his career, Onslow cites his long baseball experience. Between 1909 and 1924 he had playing service in the Texas League, the Central League, the International League, in the American League with Detroit, the National League with New York, and served stretches in the Pacific Coast League, the American Association, and the Virginia League.

He was a coach for Bill McKechnie at Pittsburgh in 1925 and 1926. He coached for Bucky Harris at Washington in 1927 and went with McKechnie to St. Louis in 1928. During 1929 he went to Newark to coach for Tris Speaker, who was the manager. At one stage Speaker left the club for a time while it was in last place. When he got back the club was in fourth place. After Newark Onslow went to the Phillies and then to Richmond, where he managed the club and took second place. He left Richmond to join Bucky Harris at Boston, and when Harris left, so did Onslow.

Then came a stage in which Onslow went into broadcasting. Being a zealous soul he went all out in preparation for his debut before the microphone. He took deep breathing, voice culture, and throat lozenges. When the great moment arrived, the commercial announcer finished his spiel and the air was all Onslow's. He burst forth to the waiting world, "Good evening, Jack Onslow! This is everybody speaking!"

After a session in radio Onslow got into the Eastern League to manage Hartford, an affiliate of the Boston Braves. During his second year there he had a run-in with Casey Stengel, then managing the Braves, and resigned. Then came his seven lean years, during which he was unable to get any kind of a baseball job.

"I finally put my pride back in my pocket and went back to the Braves," Onslow said. "I talked with Harry Jenkins, head of their farm system. He shadowboxed me for a while and then he flattened me. He couldn't give me a job, he said, because I didn't know enough people in baseball. That's the damndest, silliest rap ever given me."

In 1946 Patsy O'Rourke, then head scout for the White Sox hired Onslow to do a bit of scouting in New England. Less than a year later O'Rourke and Les O'Connor asked Onslow if he would go to Waterloo and fill in for Johnny Mostil, the manager, who was having the sixth-place blues.

Sure, Onslow would go. By that time he'd have been willing to go to Kamchatka in order to get back into baseball.

It was at Waterloo that Onslow began to make his move in the direction of Comiskey Park, though in all probability he didn't suspect it, at the time. But let this most colorful of all the White Sox managers since Kid Gleason plot his course in his own way.

"I caught up with the Waterloo club at Decatur," said

200

Onslow. "They were playing a night game. I had a meeting with the players. I told them I was just going to take a look around. I wanted to see what kind of rules they were playing. If they were my kind of rules, all right. If they weren't, I'd let them know, soon enough.

"The game was over at about a quarter of eleven. I went back to the hotel where the club stopped and had a bite to eat. I took me a seat in the lobby. No cop, mind you. Just wanted to see what happened. I sat there until three o'clock in the morning before the first group of my players came in.

"I walked over and asked them if that was the rule. They said it was. They explained that they slept all day. I changed that. Two hours after night games are enough for anybody to get a bite and relax after night games. I think that rule works. I'm no white-ribbon guy, but if my players don't use good sense then it's up to me to make them. If I can't make them, then I got to get rid of them.

"There was something else I did at Waterloo that's one of my rules. It's about pitching. I don't want any slow-ball pitchers around me, or experimenters with sliders and that trick stuff. I want my pitchers to throw hard for me or they'll be throwing for somebody else. Hell with that butterfly stuff.

"Took a little while to beat that into them at Waterloo but it finally took hold. We won thirty-five out of forty-six games, tied for third place and then won the play-off.

"After the season O'Connor told me the White Sox were dealing for the Memphis club. He signed me to a Waterloo contract but said if the Memphis deal went through I'd be the manager. I signed the contract at the Baseball Writers Dinner in New York that winter.

"I really stepped into something at Memphis. My idea was to pick players out of our own organization on their way up. Memphis sports writers didn't like that, at all. They wanted older, experienced players on the way down from the majors and the Class AAA's. They let me know I was a jerk. But I had a plan and if it didn't work out, then it was my hard luck.

"My young players caught fire. We'd been picked to finish seventh but we wound up second. We lost a pretty good outfielder named Armstrong for three weeks with a broken thumb or we might have won the pennant.

"Late in the season Chuck Comiskey came down to look the property over. We talked lots of baseball and he asked my opinion about certain things with the White Sox. I answered him, best I could. After the season he wired me to come to Chicago. I had a hunch what was on his mind, so I came in. He didn't beat around the bush. He asked me how I'd like to take over the White Sox. I said I'd like it a great deal, but for how long and for how much? He asked how much I wanted and I said all I could get. I also wanted a two year contract with an option for renewal. He named a figure that was more money than I ever got in baseball in my life."

And so Jack Onslow, night onto sixty, became the manager of the White Sox.

He reached Comiskey Park a bit ahead of Frank Lane, the general manager, which, it was soon to develop, was to be his hard luck. Though Lane's activity in organized baseball covers a span half as long as Onslow's, in his time he has encompassed enough adventures to compare favorably with the nomadic existence of "Here and There" Onslow.

For more than twenty years after leaving the University of Cincinnati Lane was a ranking football and basketball official in the Big Ten, the Southern, the Eastern, and the Ohio Conferences. He had experience as a sports editor in Cincinnati. He was assistant treasurer for a time in a New York firm of cotton brokers.

He broke into baseball in 1933 as assistant to Larry MacPhail at Cincinnati. MacPhail, most colorful of all the

202

general managers of modern times, also had training as a football official, though that is not advanced as any reason why either he or Lane were attracted to each other. Following two years with MacPhail, Lane became president of the Reds' farm club at Durham in the Piedmont League. Then he served five years as director of all Cincinnati's farm clubs.

When MacPhail became part owner of the New York Yankees Lane was made farm director for the western group of clubs in the Yankee system. He abandoned this project to become president of the American Association. In between other activities Lane helped in the reorganization of the South Atlantic, the Three Eye, and the Western leagues.

In the midst of his baseball career he enlisted in the spring of 1942 in the U. S. Navy and was commissioned as Lieutenant. He served more than a year at Corpus Christi and in 1944 was with the Air Force, Atlantic Fleet, in rank Lieutenant Commander. The following year he was with the Air Force, Pacific Fleet, rank of Commander. He had citations in each theater of operations.

Thus, as a successor to shy Les O'Connor, the White Sox came up with a man who in baseball comes as close to being all things to all people as the complete search of the whole structure of organized ball might reveal.

Within two months of their appointment Lane and Onslow had traded away several of the old familiars who had been too old or too familiar around Comiskey Park. They revised the management of several of the farm properties. They were men of action, and above all, they were ever ready with the spoken word.

Presently Onslow, offering opinions on the White Sox ways and means to interviewers in New England, was contradicting Lane who was expounding on the same subject in Chicago or elsewhere. When the press editorially called attention to this, the organization began showing marked ability for saying the same thing at the same time—but not for long.

The new policy, outlined by Lane, was that since something had to be done, there was no time like the present for doing it. The White Sox were prepared to put on the field a team materially younger than previous units and Chicago's fandom appeared to react favorably to this platform. No one expected miracles, for after all, these were still the White Sox, with an almost unbroken record of failures since 1920. Neither did anyone look for immediate cessation of incidents of the typical White Sox style.

Thus when Lane and several members of a greatly augmented Department of the Interior left for the minorleague meetings in December, 1948, the situation was ripe for another one of those things that could happen only to the White Sox.

From the meeting in Minneapolis came word that first baseman Tony Lupien had been sent to the Sacramento club of the Pacific Coast League. In order to effect such a transfer waivers had to be secured from both major leagues. Not until the announcement of Lupien's transfer was made did Lane find out that one of his underlings assigned to this clerical duty had secured waivers only from the American League. None had been asked from the National League. The process had to be undergone a second time. This time Detroit refused to waive and thus held up Lupien's transfer to the minor league. To add to the confusion Cleveland also refused to waive.

So, within a few months of taking office, Lane found out what was meant by the tradition that there were things in baseball which could happen only to the White Sox.

CHAPTER THIRTY-THREE

WHEN he took his squad to Pasadena for spring training in 1949, Jack Onslow made one promise. "We'll not finish in last place," he said. "That, I'll guarantee. How much higher we'll go will depend to some extent on the effort we show, and not as much on the breaks a lot of people like to cry about."

Onslow, in conjunction with Lane proceeded to clean house.

"Maybe," said Lane, "we had to take criticism for hanging onto some of those we did, as long as we did. It wasn't that we were being fooled. We just couldn't arrange the transfers the way we wanted it."

In discussing one of the White Sox characters who was ultimately sent to another major-league club, Lane said, "I don't care if he hits .800 for the club that's got him, now. He wasn't ever going to be a winning ball player for us, so whatever we got for him, we're that much ahead."

Onslow and his coach, Ray Berres, busied themselves with young pitchers, three of whom had reached the White Sox in trades. Long before the 1949 season was through the entire American League was marveling over the pitching of these youngsters, Bill Wight, Bill Pierce, and Bob Kuzava.

Onslow disclaimed any gift of magic. "All I kept telling them," he said, "was to get the ball over—pitch strikes—and throw hard. When I got them doing that, it was a breeze."

Not all of Onslow's newcomers justified his faith in them, which was to be expected. However, Gus Zernial, who came up from the Pacific Coast League, speedily developed into a terrific hitter and his batting exploits were the talk of the league.

For more than six weeks after the American League race started, Big Gus and his bat terrified rival pitchers. He was maintaining an average of .355. He was driving in runs galore and he was maintaining an imposing extra-base total for his wallops. Then, late in May, in the tenth inning of a ball game at Cleveland, Zernial came charging in for a low, line drive hit by Thurman Tucker. Big Gus crashed heavily when he dove for the ball, and rolled over, writhing in agony. His collar bone was broken. He was finished as a regular player for the rest of the season.

Just what the loss of Zernial meant to the White Sox for the rest of the way is conjecture, of course. However, as the club went through its schedule, it counted no less than thirty-one games which were lost by one run. Both Lane and Onslow thought it reasonable to suppose that the bat of Big Gus might have decided a fair portion of those in the White Sox favor.

Onslow did not whimper over this ill fortune. "It isn't going to bring Big Gus back," he said. "Maybe we'll have to try and do a little more with what we have left. I think most of the boys have figured that way. They're finding out they can win darn near as easy as they can lose. Maybe we'll surprise a lot of people, even without Zernial."

That, they did, for the White Sox of 1949 rose to sixth place. They played to 937,151 at Comiskey Park, a gain of 159,037 over the previous year.

The driving tactics of Onslow, the toughest White Sox

manager since Kid Gleason, was the subject of considerable comment by the press throughout the season. Onslow kept no secrets and neither did his ball players, and there was a steady succession of stories of the jawing matches between the boss and the help.

Onslow didn't seem to be too disturbed over all this. "I think I get along pretty good with the players," he said. "They're all different. You can't handle them all the same. One of my infielders, Cass Michaels, probably thinks I'm a terrible man. I'm on him, a lot. But it's the only way to get the best out of him. He can be a great ball player, but if you don't keep on him, he gets sluggish. Those kind aren't for me."

Whether he liked Onslow or disliked him, Michaels was named as the American League's All Star second baseman. He played in every game and finished with a .308 batting average which was high for the regulars. At season's end, Michaels, along with the four pitchers, Kuzava, Wight, Pierce, and Gumpert were coveted by every other American League team desirous of making deals to strengthen for the 1950 season.

"I haven't been around long enough to know," said Lane, "but some of those who have tell me this is the first time in more than twenty-five years that the other clubs have been chasing the White Sox for players. It used to be the other way around."

Michaels' batting average topped by seven points the figure turned in by Luke Appling, who played in 142 games in his nineteenth season of service with the White Sox. Partway through the season, Appling established a new major-league record for most games participated in by a shortstop. That mark had been 2,153 games, played by Rabbit Maranville in nineteen years of National League duty with Boston, Pittsburgh, Chicago, Brooklyn, and St. Louis. Appling's endurance mark was with the one club with which his entire major-league career had been identified. Having passed Maranville's mark, Appling kept right on going. At season's end he had a total of 2,198 games.

Onslow's remarkable first-year record of bringing raw material quickly to major-league standards was overlooked by many in the rush to acclaim Casey Stengel's great job in steering the New York Yankees, plagued by injuries, to a league title over the favored Boston Red Sox, and then through a decisive triumph over Brooklyn, in the world's series. Stengel, as Onslow, was one of baseball's veterans, and their outlook on procedure had many points in common.

"A lot of people tell you this game has changed a lot," Onslow said. "I don't think it has. I think most of the old-time rules for winners are as good now as they ever were.

"You hear a lot of squawking about players unable to bunt well. Years ago it wasn't like that. They just don't practice it right, any more. Watch one of those pepper games before a ball game..Man with the bat taps the ball to three or four others. That's where he should be bunting, placing the ball here and there. He doesn't. He takes swings and sends line drives and pop flies to the others. What good does that do anybody? Main object of a pepper game is to get the fielders to bend over and move around.

"Another thing you have to do is stop all these fellows from trying for a home run on every swing. They're not *all* potential home run hitters, even with the lively ball. They just think they are.

"Take a little fellow of ours, Herb Adams. As soon as I had a look at him I knew he wasn't a long-ball hitter. But he had great speed and he ought to be able to bunt and drag a ball. I sent him down to Memphis for seasoning. Told him to try at least one bunt, or drag every time he came to bat. With his speed he would get away with three of those out of ten tries. Pretty soon he'd have the infield charging on him every time he came to bat. Then he'd be able to push the ball through. I figured that would make him a real nuisance for pitchers."

When Zernial was injured Onslow recalled Adams from Memphis. The youngster, brilliantly defensive, participated in fifty-six games. He closed the season with a .293 batting average, and every time he came to bat he had opposing teams on edge wondering what he was going to do next.

In the course of the season, the White Sox came up with an eighteen-year-old prodigy, Jim Baumer, of Broken Arrow, Oklahoma. He had been sought, because of his prep-school record, by many clubs wealthier than the White Sox, but Lane's $50,000 bonus offer for the youngster's signature, was good enough to land him.

How did the White Sox happen to get him, when the much greater bank rolls of Detroit, Pittsburgh, Cleveland, and others were being waved in the face of Baumer, Sr.?

"I told the boy's father how high we would go," said Lane. "If that wasn't enough, then I was wasting his time, and he was wasting mine. He said, right off, that he liked our way of doing business. That's all there was to it."

Baumer was assigned to the Waterloo club where he fielded capably, but broke no batting records. He was recalled by the White Sox toward season's end. One afternoon in Philadelphia, Onslow decided to give the aged Appling a few innings rest, and ordered Baumer to go in at shortstop.

His major league debut was unique. It was sensational. He fainted dead away.

Reporters Ed Burns, Irving Vaughan, John Hoffman, Jim Enright, Howard Roberts, Jack Ryan, and Edgar Munzel assigned to the White Sox during the 1949 season profess to be unable to estimate the number of hours of sleep they lost trying to keep up with the frequent clashes between

Onslow and Lane. Few of the writers, by established Chicago custom, viewed the situation dispassionately. All were agreed that either Onslow or Lane would have to go.

"I got a contract that has a year to go," said Onslow. "If they don't want me—and none of the Comiskeys has told me they don't—they'll have to settle in full."

When it was recalled that Lane had a contract good for five years, Onslow became the odds on choice in the morning line to be the first to leave.

Leo Fischer, sports editor of the *Chicago Herald American,* took advantage of the situation by requesting an expression of opinion from readers on a manager for the White Sox of 1950.

The reaction to this poll was that Onslow had done a good job and was entitled to be retained, but when the votes were counted, the very popular Luke Appling, who very likely had no managerial aspirations whatever at the time, was found to have led the poll, off by himself. Thus, the Voice of the People.

When the feud between Lane and Onslow threatened to get entirely out of hand, Mrs. Grace Comiskey spoke a few well chosen words. These put everyone in his place. Everyone included Lane, Onslow, and her son Charles, who was nominal head of the organization. No peace treaty was actually signed, but during the armistice, Lane, Onslow, and the young Comiskey joined forces at the annual draft meeting and subsequently at the Minor Association assembly in Baltimore and the major-league meeting in New York. No club in either major league went through its affairs there more smoothly than the White Sox. While neither Lane nor Onslow stepped out of their bickering character for a moment, it was plain to see they were in accord on one item, a real attempt to lift the club well above the depth to which it plummeted after ill-starred 1919.

Lane and young Comiskey were to make statements

that were prophetical. For the first time in years, no pauses were being taken to count the costs. Lane resented that implication.

"I want to say," he remarked, "that I had heard a lot about that before coming to the club. I found it wasn't true, at all, and isn't now. I was genuinely amazed when I saw the salaries the White Sox were paying. I doubt if more than two or three other major-league clubs had a heavier player payroll. And you must remember that I'm not a green pea at this salary thing. I served time with the Yankees, the Reds, and elsewhere in baseball before coming here."

Young Comiskey, when not occupied in avoiding the Lane-Onslow verbal scuffles, beamed on one and all. "I think my grandfather would be proud of what we're doing," he said, "and what we intend to do, for this is only the beginning. I think Chicago's going to be proud of us, too, before many more years have passed."

But before Chicago, in 1951, was to exult for a while over the White Sox, as few cities have ever done, there had to be many more stirring on- and off-field incidents such as could not happen to anyone else but the White Sox.

CHAPTER THIRTY-FOUR

Frank Lane, very much the man in motion now, in connection with White Sox affairs, was constantly on the alert for prospects that might strengthen the club. He had heard, as most folks in baseball had, tales of a native Venezuelan, Alejandro Carrasquel, a twenty-one-year-old whose short stopping was a source of constant amazement to Texas League fans. Carrasquel, two years before, had been signed in his native Caracas to a contract which made him the property of the Brooklyn Dodger system. Fresco Thompson, the field agent of Branch Rickey's far flung Dodger empire, had signed Carrasquel to a Montreal contract. The youngster, along with scores of others, appeared in the Dodger camp in Florida in the spring of 1948. It developed that Montreal had no pressing need for a shortstop, but Fort Worth, another Dodger farm club, did. So to Fort Worth went Carrasquel, able to speak little or no English, but gifted with fielding skill seldom visited upon a shortstop.

Many a major-league scout, patrolling the Texas League beat, looked with envious eyes upon Carrasquel, but did no more about it. He was Fort Worth property. Fort Worth was Dodger property. Dodger property meant Branch Rickey, shrewdest trader of them all. Certainly there would be no purpose trying to talk Rickey out of a prospect such as that, whatever the price. That's the way all major-league trade makers but one viewed it. The one who demurred was Frank Lane.

Brooklyn, in the Rickey regime—he has since gone over to the Pittsburgh Pirates—controlled players of all kinds. It was perfectly natural for Lane, the shopper, to have a session with Rickey, as he did following the 1949 season.

Rickey, by custom, had bargains galore, in which Lane was not interested, but he listened to the sales talk, just the same. Quite accidentally, Lane was able to introduce the name of Carrasquel into the conversation. Rickey was aghast that anyone would have the temerity to suppose that he would yield title to Carrasquel. He talked fast, but for the first time in his trading career, he had found pitted against him one who was equally quick on the conversation and every bit as persistent.

In an unguarded moment, while outlining his long list of bargains, Rickey inadvertently put a price on Carrasquel. Lane noted it, but said nothing, and presently the session ended. Next day Lane sent Rickey a telegram from New York to Brooklyn, stating that the Chicago White Sox had accepted the terms for Carrasquel and would take him.

Then he sat back and awaited developments. They were not long in coming. Rickey got on the phone and argued that he had not agreed to sell Carrasquel, but had merely put a price on him, subject to his own reservation, if he saw fit. He saw fit. He had fits. But at the other end of the phone, the gifted gabster, Lane, calmly insisted that this wasn't the way he'd heard it. A legitimate offer had been made. It had been accepted in good faith. Rickey was an honorable man, whose word was as good as his bond. Lane was an honorable man, who trusted the word of Rickey. It was all as simple as that. Perhaps for the first time in his trading career which he had begun at St. Louis, and carried through at Brooklyn, Rickey had met his master.

Carrasquel was White Sox property, for a price generally accepted as $25,000 and two waiver-price ball players, the waiver price being $10,000. The players were shortstop Fred Hancock and pitcher Charles Eisenmann. Hancock balked at going where Rickey chose to send him and Lane promptly wrote a check for $10,000 which Rickey was able to send anywhere he cared.

The legend of Carrasquel was such that this deal, for Chicago consumption, threatened to get more space than had been accorded years ago when Rickey, then at St. Louis, was persuaded to send Dizzy Dean to the Cubs for $185,000, some players, and a quit claim to any and all headaches the inimitable Dean might cause in what was left of his baseball future.

Carrasquel's joining the White Sox now presented the spring training camp at Pasadena with two situations which observers had to regard twenty-four hours a day. The Lane-Onslow feud was still bubbling. Now, there was another one in the making.

If Carrasquel were the kind of a shortstop everyone seemed to think he was, what about the veteran Luke Appling, who had been the White Sox shortstop as long, it sometimes seemed, as the memory of man?

It was something which Appling did not choose to worry about much, at first. In his nineteen seasons with the White Sox, he had come to camp many other springs, preceded by tales of remarkable young men who were going to take his job away. When the season opened, Appling was the shortstop, and Old Aches and Pains wasn't immediately concerned with this newcomer, though he did show a marked interest in the youngster's work, and tried to be most helpful to him.

Carrasquel, unable to speak English, was fortunate in

having as a teammate pitcher Luis Aloma, up from Buffalo. Aloma not only spoke English, but he spoke Spanish. It was agreed that, once Carrasquel caught on, as he did from the instant he first appeared at Pasadena, Aloma was sure of a job, whether he could pitch, or not. As a matter of fact Aloma was not only a first-class interpreter, but he developed into one of the American League's first relief pitchers. When the story of his career is finally written it will be discovered that the help he has given fellow pitchers in their moments of distress was as great as any linguistic aid he has given a fellow Latin American.

Before the 1950 spring exhibition season was fairly launched, Onslow let it be known that Carrasquel was to be the White Sox shortstop.

But what of Appling?

"He's going to be my first baseman," said Onslow.

That, as the saying goes, is what Onslow thought. What Appling thought, and what Appling said, was something else again.

He did make a pass at working out at first base, but he had been on the other side of the diamond too many years to become a George Sisler in a few weeks. The number of Old Aches and Pains was up. He was a fixture in the White Sox organization, as well he might be, but from the moment Chico Carrasquel arrived at Pasadena, Appling's playing days were numbered. He held on as a coach, and at season's end, when offered the job of managing the White Sox farm at Memphis, surprised everyone, including himself, by accepting it.

If the Carrasquel deal took precedence over anything else in Lane's activity between the close of the 1949 season and the start of 1950's, that does not argue that he had been idle the rest of the time. From the moment he took desk space at Comiskey Park, Lane had been routing players in and out of the White Sox organization.

Some of his machinations were complicated. Catcher Joe Tipton had been obtained from Cleveland for pitcher Joe Haynes. Tipton and Onslow did not see eye to eye on many matters, so Lane traded him to Philadelphia for second baseman Nelson Fox, whose physical proportions were more nearly those of a steeplechase rider than of a rugged major-league infielder. But Fox is a name to remember.

Interpreter and relief man Aloma had been drafted from Buffalo. Pitcher Ken Holcombe had been brought from Sacramento. Catcher Phil Masi was bought from Pittsburgh.

A typical Lane transaction was one in which Don Kolloway, long a White Sox favorite, went to Detroit for Earl Rapp and $15,000. Rapp and $20,000 went to Oakland for George Metkovich, and Metkovich was resold to Oakland for $25,000.

Another found him taking pitcher Ed Klieman from New York on waivers and subsequently trading him to the Athletics for third baseman Hank Majeski. There were many other deals, but Lane was merely warming up. The big ones were ahead.

If he had a program in the spring of 1950, and it is to be assumed he had, its principal planks were (a) get rid of Onslow and select a manager of his own choosing; (b) obtain a hitting first baseman; (c) obtain some outfielders who could hit, run, and throw. Before the 1950 season was well under way, Lane had reached two of his objectives.

The White Sox were away to a dull start, and toward the end of May they had lost almost three times as many games as they had won. Warfare between Lane and Onslow had broken out anew, and day by day the press and the public stood by for the long awaited explosion that would carry one or the other, perhaps both, away.

Following a night game late in May—the White Sox had

now a record of eight won and twenty-two lost—the base-ball writers were told that Onslow would serve out the rest of his $20,000 contract, but serve it somewhere else than at Comiskey Park.

What Onslow had to say about this and about Lane, and what Lane had to say about that and about Onslow must be left to the reader's imagination. Actually, the situation had been such that the news that one of these clashing-by-nature personalities was on his way, came as a relief to the Chicago public as well as to the reporters who had been trying to keep up with it.

For a time there was a great deal said on both sides. The Onslow adherents, of which there were many, insisted that he had done an excellent job in his first year, and that his troubles were chiefly due to Lane's interference. It was even suggested that Lane become field as well as general manager, and see how long he would last.

The Comiskeys, Mrs. Grace, and Charles II, the nominal head of the organization, were somewhat aloof from the uproar. It was to be supposed that they, too, were satisfied that if nothing else had been accomplished, conversation for publication at Comiskey Park had been trimmed in half. That was a distinct gain.

In such confusion as reigned, Coach John Corriden, a baseball veteran, agreed to handle the club for the rest of the season. Manager pro tem Corriden, in all his years in baseball, had never indulged in language stronger than "Jiminy gosh!" He accepted the mantle thrown over his shoulders in the wee, small hours of that May morning. He accepted it for better, or for worse.

As it turned out, it was for worse.

The White Sox of 1950, while holding their sixth place in the American League race, to which Onslow had lifted them the year before, nevertheless played to but 781,330 as contrasted with the 937,151 of the year 1949.

But in that weirdly wonderful season, Lane managed to gain his first and second objectives, and was already drawing of plans to reach his third. One day pitcher Bob Kuzava, second baseman Cass Michaels, and Pitcher John Ostrowski were bundled up and sent to Washington for pitcher Ray Scarborough, who specialized in annoying the Boston Red Sox, for second baseman Al Kozar, and for the long awaited first baseman, Eddie Robinson.

Despite the attendance slump, and the failure of the club to make yards upward in the American League race, Lane was still the busy businessman, and cheering him on was young Comiskey.

Neither had lost sight of the fact that John Corriden was not to stay as manager for 1951. Nor had the public. Great was the speculation on the identity of the next in line. Few guessed correctly.

The one Lane had in mind from the time he accepted a five-year contract as the White Sox general manager, was Paul Richards, who had served in the 1950 season as manager of the Seattle club. When Lane thought the proper time had arrived, he summoned his man. Though few suspected it at the time, the greatest year in modern White Sox history was in the making.

CHAPTER THIRTY-FIVE

PAUL RICHARDS, as a small boy in his native Waxahachie, Texas, had his first glimpse of Chicago White Sox in a spring when Manager Kid Gleason had the club train there. A legend has developed that the Kid, in a playful mood, one day chased young Richards off the field and into the stands.

Perhaps an imaginative radio script man or movie scenarist would deduce from that that Richards was destined for the White Sox. Richards himself, an able writer— he, too, was once a sports writer—doesn't think so. Nor should he.

His baseball career, which began in the Eastern Shore League in 1926, betook him to such places as Waterbury, Muskogee, Asheville, and Macon by easy stages. He caught three games for Brooklyn in 1932. He was with the New York Giants in 1933, having come up from Minneapolis. In the years 1936 through 1942 he caught for and managed the Atlanta club, winning two pennants, and one post-season play-off. From 1943 through 1946 he caught for and coached Detroit. He went to Buffalo as manager in 1947, and while there also served as general manager, winning a pennant in 1949. He went to Seattle for the 1950 season, no doubt to have something to do while Frank Lane fought his winning battle against Jack Onslow. For even then, Richards knew he was to lead the White Sox in 1951.

So much for a sketch of the Richards' travelogue.

Of all those places and dates, the ones pertinent to this story are Macon, and perhaps, Detroit and the year 1945. It was at Macon that Lane first glimpsed Richards. He was a pitcher then, and ambidextrous, no less. While Lane watched a double-header, and recalled that Dick Merriwell was the only pitcher he had ever heard of who threw strikes with either hand, Richards appeared at third base in the second game. Some further investigation disclosed that he had also played second base, first base, and short-stop.

Lane was so impressed he communicated with Larry MacPhail, then president of the Columbus American Association club and recommended Richards. McPhail wasn't particularly excited about it, but passed the information on to Mike Kelly of Minneapolis, who took the young man on, and eventually peddled him to the Giants.

During Lane's term as farm director for the Cincinnati Reds, Birmingham was one of their properties. Birmingham was in the same league as Atlanta, where Richards caught and managed, and Lane had ample chance to watch him.

"He had added something else to his repertoire by this time," Lane recalls. "Now he not only managed and caught, but he insisted on umpiring all the games he caught. He was the sort of a firebrand you'd hate, but one you'd like to have on your side, just the same.

"I saw some more of him at Buffalo, and I decided then that if the time ever came when I wanted a manager, Paul Richards would be my man.

"He is my man with the White Sox for two reasons. First, he is certainly qualified on all counts. And second, he helps follow out an idea I've always had. That is, that it's sound practice to give a major-league managerial chance to one who has qualified in the minors, rather than to select someone who has had major-league managing experience. I contend that the very fact that a man has managed another major-league club, or several, is sufficient proof that he isn't the kind I'd want. If he were, he simply wouldn't be available. The club that had first search on him wouldn't have let him go."

You were advised to remember the place, Detroit. It was as a member of the Detroit Tigers that catcher Paul Richards participated in the world's series of 1945, and became a figure more familiar to Chicago than he had been in any of his previous regular season visits.

This 1945 set of post-season games, had been properly characterized as the world's worst series. Prior to its opening, this author was among the many correspondents polled for an opinion as to the probable winner by the Associated Press. His reply, which gained more than passing attention, was, "I don't think either one of them can win it."

This pregame opinion became almost literally true. Cubs and Tigers went from the sublime (Claude Passeau's marvelous one-hit shutout in the third game) to the ridiculous Chicago 8, Detroit 7 sixth game, and the 9 to 3 seventh game which gave the series to Detroit.

Truly, it appeared as if neither could, or would win it, but in that final game it was a hit by Paul Richards which turned the balance, such as it was, in Detroit's favor.

Thus it was, that when Richards, in the winter months of 1951 made one of his first Chicago public appearances at the annual Baseball Writers Diamond Dinner, the toastmaster, in introducing him, said that for too long he had waited to acknowledge a debt of gratitude to Richards.

221

"If it were not for you," he said, "that 1945 series might still be going on."

Richards and Lane were in perfect accord from the start. They spent many hours in going over the White Sox needs. Richards was firm in his belief that the large Comiskey Park was no place for the slow of foot. Speed and more speed was what was needed. And defense. "One of the primary objects of the game," said Richards, "is to get the other side out."

He had been impressed, he said, with the speed of outfielder Jim Busby, who had been with Sacramento in the Pacific Coast League, and who was recalled for 1951 survey.

"I saw another fellow out there," he said. "He was with San Diego. That Orestes Minoso, who belongs to Cleveland. No price would be too great for him."

Minoso, a Negro player from Cuba, had been surveyed by Cleveland, but there seemed some doubt whether he was a third baseman or an outfielder. Lane made a point of that.

"Get him," said Richards, "if you can. I'll find a place to play him."

Easier said than done, but Lane was willing to give it a try. Meanwhile there was other business to be done.

The Boston Red Sox craved pitchers, of which the White Sox now possessed many. They were openly courted by Lane during the December baseball meetings. Out of much discussion came one of the most important wholesale player transactions in Lane's career, up to that time.

Pitcher Ray Scarborough, the one who specialized in beating the Red Sox, appealed to Boston trade maker Joe Cronin, who felt it was better to have Scarborough with him than against him. Lane was willing. Bill Wight, reputed one of the league's best young prospects was craved by Boston. Lane would want something substantial for him. How about Al Zarilla? The latter had been purchased from St. Louis for some of those boxcar figures associated with the wealthy Red Sox transactions. He had been a regular member of the outfield, but Cronin said he could be had, and pitcher Joe Dobson with him, for Wight and Scarborough.

Lane considered that a while. It wasn't enough, in his judgment. The Red Sox finally consented to toss in another young pitcher, Dick Littlefield. The deal was consummated on that basis.

It was hinted that while Zarilla gave new manager Richards another fleet-footed outfielder, base runner, and batsman, and that the veteran Dobson might compensate for the loss of Scarborough and Wight, the youngster, Littlefield, was really the "sleeper" in the deal. If so, the young man was still somewhat somnolent as these chapters of White Sox history reach a climax.

The White Sox squad turned over to Richards at Pasadena in the spring of 1951 bore some resemblance to the outfit which had faltered in 1950, unable to improve its sixth place in the pennant race. The manager, to all of the squad save those who had played for him somewhere along the line, was something entirely new.

Richards, beyond a doubt, was major-league baseball's hardest-working manager. His players soon found that training under his direction was something that began early and finished late, with very little, if any, time off for good behavior.

Richards had never seen Carrasquel, prior to glimpsing him at Pasadena. There had been some alarm over Carrasquel's condition, for after the 1950 season he had submitted to an operation for the removal of torn cartilage, a relic of a knee injury. However, Chico said he was all right—and said it in English, too. During the winter months in Venezuela he had patronized North American players to such an extent that he was no longer dependent on Luis Aloma to make with the language for him. In a few brief whirls through infield and batting drills Richards was convinced that all he had heard of Carrasquel was true. This might well be the shortstop of all time, before his career was done.

Meanwhile Richards turned his attention to Fox, the tiny second baseman, whose .247 batting average in 130 games had disturbed no pitcher's peace of mind in 1950. Richards, and his coach, Doc Cramer, made some marked changes in the style and the type of bat Fox used. Progress was immediate, and then was sensational. In Fox, Richards found a kindred spirit. "Little Nell" instead of wearing away to a shadow from his generous estimate of 150 pounds or so playing weight actually thrived on hard work.

Richards had his shortstop now, and his second baseman. He hoped to rekindle in first baseman Robinson a spark that had been lacking ever since the Cleveland club, his first major-league affiliate, began shunting him around. Richards had his first baseman, if Robinson came through as a steady workman.

Third baseman? Anything new on the Minoso deal? No one but Lane and Richards knew that such a deal was even in the blueprint stage.

Work went on at the Pasadena camp, and finally the spring exhibition games began. The White Sox were in shape. They couldn't help but be, with the amount of work Richards gave them. He was here, there, and everywhere. The White Sox would be scheduled to play an exhibition game at Wrigley Field, Los Angeles, in the morning. Part of the squad would remain at the Pasadena camp for a morning workout. The others would take the bus to Los Angeles. Richards would remain at Pasadena, direct the camp drill, and then drive to Los Angeles to direct his team in the afternoon.

Did the team look badly in the game? If so, more often

224

than not, after the nine innings were played, the lads were kept in after school for more practice.

That was the vogue all along the spring training exhibition route, if train catching schedules permitted the after-school exercises. And never once did Richards delegate the work to his coaches while he dressed and sought the nearest rare steak. No, indeed, he was the last one to leave the field.

Evidence was given of this along the spring exhibition route. Nor was it withheld when the White Sox reached Chicago and happened to blow a game at Comiskey Park in the annual spring series with their cross-town rival Cubs.

Even the bat boy was kept after school that day. So strenuous was the batting and fielding drill given the White Sox in the gathering shadows of that chilly April afternoon, *Daily News* sports editor, John Carmichael, a White Sox and American League advocate from 'way back, was moved to ask if Richards were starting spring training all over again.

The deadly earnestness of this newest of the White Sox managers and his burning desire for perfection in every game, exhibition or regular season, was something new for Chicago fans. There was none of the "let's get 'em tomorrow" about Richards. His platform was to get 'em today, and if his club didn't, he proposed to let it know why, before any considerable time had elapsed.

The skeptics insisted that his rigorous schedule must wear the White Sox squad out, long before the American League season had completed its 154 string of games. The skeptics were wrong. Another school of thought theorized that Richards must wind up with at least a few ball players rebellious at the sort of no-rest-for-the-weary treatment. This school of thought was off the beam, too.

The White Sox ranged through a lengthy spring exhibition series with a record that surpassed any compiled by the accepted major-league powers, Yankees, Indians, Red Sox, Dodgers, and Giants. The White Sox were the Grapefruit League champions. They were getting themselves talked about at home and abroad. True, there was an undercurrent—could they keep it up?

With what they had then, perhaps not. But Richards knew what he still needed to fashion the club into a unit that, barring crippling injuries to its key men, might be in the race all the way.

After its long dearth of first-division baseball Chicago was eager to take either of its clubs on trust, and the White Sox, for a long time, not only did not let its fans down, but actually exceeded their fondest expectations.

The Cubs—who were again destined to plumb the depths of the National League, and eventually cause Manager Frank Frisch to retire in midseason—now had patronage competition in Chicago for the first time since the more than a million attendance marks became the order of the Wrigley Field season, regardless of the Cubs' position in the pennant race.

The White Sox were away to a brisk start. Their team speed, their aggressiveness, and above all their excellent conditioning, sustained them through the opening weeks. The pitching was surprisingly good. But Richards wanted more speed and more pitching, and to get both, Frank Lane established a new major-league record for long-distance telephone conversation.

On the last day of April he was in the Hotel Commodore in New York. He had been sequestered there for thirty-six hours, practically doing nothing else but making or accepting long distance calls. When he hung up the phone for the last time, it was after having told Richards that the man he wanted, Orestes Minoso, was now White Sox property.

226

Announcement of this deal created a sensation in Chicago, not only for what Minoso's undoubted talent might do to accelerate the White Sox pace that was already demoralizing the opposition, but for the fact that Chicago now had its first Negro player ready for major-league duty. Others had been signed previously, but were still in minor leagues undergoing needed training.

The deal which brought Minoso to Chicago was quite complicated. To complete it, Lane had to become middleman in a proposed transaction between Cleveland and Philadelphia, which, at first was none of his concern whatever.

Hank Greenberg, big dealer for Cleveland, in conjunction with Manager Al Lopez, was certain that in the stout arms of Bob Feller, Bob Lemon, Early Wynn, Mike Garcia, and perhaps Steve Gromek, the Indians would not lack for starting pitchers. But a relief man was needed. Lou Brissie, of the Athletics, was the man Cleveland coveted.

General manager Arthur Ehlers of the A's, and Manager Jimmy Dykes were willing, up to a certain point. Sure, the Indians were welcome to Brissie, but pitcher Sam Zoldak, catcher Ray Murray, and the bundle of cash Greenberg offered wasn't quite enough. Dykes, no tyro at driving a sharp trading bargain, as he had proven many times while serving his long term as White Sox manager, wanted a long-ball hitter.

The long-ball hitter the Indians did not have, or at least, those they had, they did not choose to let go, even for Brissie.

That was where Frank Lane came in.

Gus Zernial was a long-ball hitter, but in Richards' appraisal, Gus left something to be desired in speed and in defensive ability. Lane suspected that Dykes would like to have Gus banging away for his side at that convenient left-field pavilion in Shibe Park. Lane's suspicions were correct. The end of the thirty-six hours of long-distance phoning resulted in the formal announcement that the Athletics had obtained Zernial and Dave Philley from the White Sox, Zoldak, Murray, and cash from the Indians, and Brissie had become Cleveland property. For the purposes of this story the main item was that Minoso had reached Chicago. Along with him came Paul Lehner, of the Athletics, but never mind about him, unless to note that at season's end he was at Cleveland, having been claimed on waivers from the St. Louis Browns, to whom the White Sox had sent him in a deal for Don Lehnhardt.

Richards was elated at the deal. "It's the best we've ever made," he said. "I wouldn't trade Minoso for anyone in the league. He has great batting power. He has tremendous speed. He can play almost any place in the line-up. Above all, he puts winning a ball game above everything, including his own personal record. I found that out about him in the Coast League, soon after Cleveland farmed him there. He was introduced to a major-league scout before the first game of a double-header. The scout, wanting to say something nice, expressed hope that Minny would get seven hits in the two games. Minoso just grinned and said he'd be satisfied with just two hits—providing each one drove in the winning run. I know Chicago's going to like Minny."

And Chicago has, from the very start. Once he had been traded to the White Sox, Minoso wasted no time at all in getting into action with his new club. He reported for duty on May 1, and in his first time at bat, hit a 425-foot homer. Not even Zernial in his fiercest moment had ever hit one harder or farther in the interests of the White Sox.

With his arrival, the White Sox were off and running, but now, for the first time since 1920, they had a general idea of both why and where.

CHAPTER THIRTY-SIX

THE slogan of the White Sox was speed, and more speed. By June 2, with Minoso, Jim Busby, and Chico Carrasquel setting the pace, they had stolen thirty bases, whereas the 1950 White Sox had stolen but nineteen for the entire season.

The fans flocking into Comiskey Park as they had never done before, soon acquired a battle cry, which was sounded as soon as the first White Sox got on base, in a game.

The stands resounded with the thunderous: "Go! Go! Sox!" And Go! the Sox did.

They raced around the bases, demoralizing other American League defenses. They ranged around the outfield, making one seemingly impossible catch after another. Given support of this spectacular sort, pitchers who were dubious qualities before now turned in one astonishing winning performance after another. Among these were Ken Holcombe, Lou Kretlow, and Harry Dorish, but among all the efficient White Sox hurlers—including Billy Pierce, Randy Gumpert, and Howie Judson—Saul Rogovin was the one whose masterful performances caused the inspired sports writers to stress what they called the Miracle of 35th Street.

Richards had known Rogovin at Buffalo, before the pitcher went up to Detroit, where his entire 1950 career had fashioned an unimpressive two and two record for the Tigers. Even while Richards was urging Frank Lane to get him Minoso, he was also asking that a deal be made for Rogovin.

At the time the deal was made, Rogovin had a one and one record at Detroit, which may not have appealed to Lane's trading sense. But Richards wanted him, and that was good enough for Lane. He made the deal, but in doing so had to give up Bob Cain, one of the most promising of the White Sox pitchers.

Cain was a Comiskey Park favorite, so the second guessing on this deal was not long in forthcoming.

Richards took it all. "I know what Saul can do," he said.

What Saul did for the White Sox made pitching history of sorts, in 1951. The Miracle wrought in Rogovin made Richards' other magic seem of the parlor sort, and soon some of the very ones who had mourned the passing of Cain for the doubtful Tiger, were saying that it would be a long time before Lane would be able to get Detroit to trade with him again.

Meanwhile the mad scramble of the White Sox was going on at top speed. Typical of the dash was a job done by Busby in a game against Detroit. He singled. He stole second. He stole third as the stands rocked to the "Go! Go! Sox!" battle cry. He scored on a squeeze play.

Chicago newspapers were now struggling to outdo each other in the proper presentation of the White Sox. The *Herald American* conceived the idea of having lapel buttons and car stickers made with the White Sox insignia and the "Go! Go! Sox!" emblazoned thereon. Demand for these fan-loyalty displays exceeded the response to any similar promotional venture in memory.

230

How long could they keep it up? The answer was not given immediately.

On their first eastern trip of the season, the White Sox visited New York, Boston, Philadelphia, Washington, and Cleveland. Game after game was racked up, most of them in sensational style. They returned home with a record of having won every game on the trip. This achievement touched off a new hysterical outburst, now no longer only in Chicago, but throughout the baseball world. They broke into the newsreels and the national magazines. In Chicago they kept the Korean situation off the front pages. Presently they were in first place, apparently geared to stay there for a while.

Neither Richards nor Lane was content with past or present success. Both kept looking into the future, and from time to time, players were dropped, and others were added, each to help perfect the club.

When the White Sox were resting in first place on July 4, it was Chicago's idea that Richards be acclaimed Manager of the Year without waiting for the formality of the season's end.

The White Sox were in first place when the midsummer pause for the annual All Star Game was taken. On the starting line-up, voted by fans the country over, Chico Carrasquel and Nellie Fox were accorded positions.

As early as May 20, Phil Rizzuto, Yankee shortstop, long regarded as his league's best at the position, found himself being quoted, "There's no doubt about it, Carrasquel is the best shortstop around."

Carrasquel, being nothing if not modest, shrugged that off with, "The best shortstop—Rizzuto, heem."

But for All Star Game purposes, the fans put Carrasquel ahead of Rizzuto.

Fox, the .247 hitter of 1950, was battling Minoso for the league's leadership in batting at All Star Game time, which seemed to many to be another of those Miracles of 35th Street.

The galaxy of White Sox stars did no better and no worse than their American League company in that 1951 All Star Game. Stan Musial, Gil Hodges, Ralph Kiner, Bob Elliott, and others showed the American League pitchers what batting power really was, for a welcome change to the National League's long suffering president, Ford Frick.

While the stellar White Sox performers were at Detroit, the remainder of the squad went out to Comiskey Park, and from force of habit, took a fall out of the Cubs, who were at full war strength.

Richards remained home to direct this one, and in the eyes of his public, this victory more than atoned for the defeat the Cubs had put upon him during the spring series.

At this stage of the season, rival managers Casey Stengel, Steve O'Neill, and Al Lopez were more than willing to accept Richards and his White Sox as a real menace.

The question was no longer, "How long can they keep it up?" but "Who's going to catch them?"

Richards kept right on giving them things to worry about. His peak was reached in a game against the Red Sox in which pitcher Harry Dorish, a right-hander, was doing well enough until a crisis was reached.

The crisis was represented by Red Sox runners in scoring position, with Ted Williams coming up to bat. Richards did not want to take Dorish out. Neither did he want him to pitch to Williams. The White Sox, at the time, had an abundance of third basemen. So Richards took his third baseman out, assigned Dorish to third, so he could remain in the game, and brought in a left-hander, Billy Pierce, to work on Williams. Pierce caused Williams to pop to

232

the shortstop, Dorish returned to the box, and a new third baseman took over for the White Sox.

Bush league! snorted the critics. That's something you'd see only on a sand lot. But the point was, it worked.

The multiplicity of White Sox third basemen, which included Minoso, Floyd Baker, and at one time, Hank Majeski, also featured Bob Dillinger, a wanderer of baseball's wastelands. He had all the elements of greatness when he broke in with the St. Louis Browns, but took his own time about using them. He was sold to the Athletics and after shedding his listless light on that scene for a while, got over into the National League with the Pittsburgh Pirates. There, much to Manager Bill Meyer's dismay, he was just one more tired man added to those the sorely tried manager already owned.

When Lane made a deal to bring Dillinger to the White Sox there was considerable debate on the motive which had prompted it. The obvious one was that Dillinger had begun his career as a base-running genius and base runners were strictly in line with Richards' policy. But Dillinger had apparently long since stopped moving around with any reckless abandon.

The attempted explanations of this deal were many. One that caught the popular fancy was that ever since Lane had talked Branch Rickey (then of Brooklyn) out of Chico Carrasquel, Rickey had been plotting to get even with him. Now, he had. As the Pittsburgh director of players' comings and goings, he had sold Lane Dillinger, tying the score.

This gag misfired when Dillinger caught the spirit of the White Sox. He proved to be a useful, if not sensational bit of property. No longer were rival bench jockeys yelling at him that if he didn't start moving around, someone would hitch a horse to him. For Richards, even a Dillinger moves around, or he moves out.

The first indication the White Sox had that fortune could be bad as well as good, came in a game at Philadelphia on June 15. Elmer Valo of the A's crashed heavily into the White Sox catcher, Gus Niarhos, and injured him badly. A free-for-all was precipitated, in which pitcher Saul Rogovin punched Valo on the nose. For this he was subsequently fined $150 by American League president, Will Harridge.

With Niarhos out of action for a while, the club was deprived of its top catcher. The other, veteran Phil Masi, was at the brittle stage, and presently the White Sox were hard pressed for catchers.

However, their momentum was to carry them for a while, even though, one day soon after the All Star Game, they looked around and there were those Yankees in again, and Red Sox and Indians not far away.

The Red Sox they could handle, though on two successive nights at Comiskey Park they seemed to be overdoing it. On July 13 they went nineteen innings to win, 5 to 4, having spent the previous night playing seventeen innings against the same club, to lose by the same score. Rogovin, the mighty man, was mixed up in one of those, thus removing any lingering doubt as to his durability.

In a game July 16, Niarhos broke his right wrist, to be lost to the club indefinitely.

Others in the cast, notably Minoso, who had become a favorite target for pitched balls, were in and out of the line-up because of injuries, but the beginning of the end of the pennant drive, at least for 1951, was in sight. Not all the heroics were over, however.

On July 18, Chico Carrasquel, in a game against the Yankees, booted a roller from Gene Woodling. This marked the first error Carrasquel had made in 298 chances. His 297 chances handled in fifty-three games, was the league's record. Carrasquel had succeeded to that when he had handled 289 chances in fifty-one games, surpassing the previous standard of 288 chances in fifty-eight games established by Phil Rizzuto.

The Yankees, as became world's champions, had accepted the challenge hurled at them by these upstart White Sox. Out of this rivalry, bitter at times, there arose a Chicago vs. New York baseball situation such as had not been known since the early years of the century when Frank Chance's Cubs and John McGraw's Giants hated the very sight and thought of each other.

Such rivalry, of course, made for gate receipts. It was no surprise then when on the night of June 8, with the Yankees visiting Comiskey Park, 53,940 were within the gates, the largest crowd in Chicago's baseball history. A day game high of 53,325 had been recorded on May 15, 1949. On August 13, 1948, on a night when Satchel Paige had been advertised as the Cleveland pitcher, 51,599 came out to see him do it—which Satch did, 1 to 0.

As matters developed however, it was not the Yankees, but the Washington Senators, who put the quietus on the White Sox hopes for 1951, even though it was not accepted as such, at the time.

On July 20, the White Sox were tied for the lead, and expected to improve their position in a four-game series with Washington at Comiskey Park. In the first game they were leading 1 to 0, with two out in the ninth. They lost the lead. They lost the game. They lost the next three with the Senators, a team they had been beating as a matter of course, until then.

They were never again in first place in the 1951 season, though it was sometime thereafter, before anyone was willing to count them out of the pennant race. And even if they were removed at last from championship consideration, there was yet in store for them many an exciting moment, including some with the Yankees which made any of their previous Donnybrooks seem like a children's party.

CHAPTER THIRTY-SEVEN

IF there has been any attempt to set up a theme song for this story of the White Sox, it has been that in all the years of their existence, things have happened to them that seldom, if ever have happened to other clubs in baseball.

The resurgent White Sox of 1951 were singularly free from this, but they were no more immune than any of their predecessors. Their turn came on the night of July 27, when the White Sox were in the Yankee Stadium. In the pennant race, the White Sox, not yet shaken off, were three and one-half games behind the leading Yankees.

Going into the ninth inning, the Yankees were leading, 3 to 1. The weather was threatening, and in the White Sox half of the ninth, after they had scored one run, rainfall caused a delay of twenty-six minutes. When play was resumed, the White Sox kept on the attack, and though Yankee Manager Casey Stengel made frequent pitching changes, the White Sox had two more runs in, were now leading 4 to 3, had the bases filled with only one out, when umpire in chief, Hank Soar, called another halt.

Richards raved and ranted at this, as he had been while Stengel, obviously stalling, used up precious minutes of time to make his pitching changes. If it had been Casey's wish to have the game called before completion, with the score, under baseball rules, thus reverting to the eighth inning, to become a Yankee 3 to 1 victory, instead of a quite possible defeat, his prayers were answered. After a wait of sixty-two minutes, Umpire Soar called the game off, and it went into the book as a Yankee victory.

However, the incident had just begun. As the night wore on, Richards became more violent in his statements over the injustice he felt had been done him. In Chicago, American League President Will Harridge, convalescing from a serious operation, was unable to see or hear immediately all the vitriolic statements this incident precipitated. Richards himself filed a 150-word protest to the league office, demanding that the game be finished at a future date before it became official.

Lane, who had remained in Chicago, heard Richards' testimony over the long-distance phone and the next morning he issued a statement which made all the front pages. It read:

> The stalling tactics of the New York club, officially established by Umpire Bill McGowan's banishment of New York third baseman Gil McDougald, when he [McDougald] refused to return to his position, should definitely direct American League President Will Harridge to the justice of Paul Richards' protest that Umpire-in-chief Hank Soar ineptly handled the situation.
>
> Several instances of stalling by the players, by Manager Casey Stengel, when he used almost one pitcher for each batter in the first half of the ninth, and the fact that pitcher Frank Shea consumed nine minutes in coming from the bullpen to the mound in the rain support Richards' protest.
>
> Likewise the statement by Soar to Richards—"They won't get away with a thing. We'll play all night, if necessary"—add justification to the protest.

Then at 12:33 A.M. (EDT) Soar called the game, saying that President Harridge does not wish to keep the fans up all night at a game. This coming after two games of last week (the seventeen- and nineteen-inning games with Boston) were concluded in the vicinity of 1:20 A.M. (CDT).

Not only has the Chicago club been denied a possible victory, but the decision by Soar also violates the rights of the Boston and Cleveland clubs. [Boston and Cleveland were then in second place, a game behind the Yankees.] A more able umpire would not have permitted the situation to get out of hand. A threatened forfeiture by the umpire would have eliminated the stalling tactics and would have brought the game to its rightful conclusion.

The Chicago club is asking for resumption of the game in the first half of the ninth inning, Chicago leading 4 to 3, bases loaded and one out.

The rain which Umpire Soar deemed too severe to permit continuance of play, subsided 10 minutes after he had called the game, and it did not rain again in New York for an hour and five minutes.

To this, as well as to other equally virulent if not as official protests, President Harridge had no reply, save that he would await the report of his umpires.

For several days, this situation was as frenzied as any in which the White Sox had ever been involved. The Chicago newspapers made an issue of it. One of them elicited a lengthy opinion from A. B. Chandler. The former commissioner had been retired to private life a few weeks previous, when he failed to ride out the storm roused by major-league executives who did not fancy his way of conducting the office. Chandler's opinion, under the circumstances, had every bit as much authority as those of Constant Reader, Joe Subscriber, and A. Fan, who were not only deluging the newspapers but the office of President Harridge with supercharged invectives.

In due time, President Harridge announced that testimony from both sides would be taken when the Yankees came to Chicago on their final western swing of the season. Long before the date set, the furor had died away. The slump into which the White Sox had fallen had taken them right out of championship consideration, leaving the hated Yankees, the Cleveland Indians, and the Boston Red Sox in a three-way stretch for the pennant.

Meanwhile retributive justice of sorts had caught up with the Yankees. One of their own late-inning rallies at Philadelphia, which would have given them victory over, instead of defeat by Jimmy Dykes' Athletics, went for naught. Rainfall on that occasion washed out the Yankees' hits and runs just as effectively as it had done for the White Sox.

The promised taking of testimony at Chicago was canceled because of the death of Manager Richards' daughter. Instead, there came a formal review and statement by President Harridge. He gave the only decision possible, the one that has been in the book as long as there has been baseball. The score at the end of eight complete innings, New York, 3; Chicago, 1, was the final and official result.

In passing President Harridge reprimanded Richards for his castigation of the league's umpires, the league, and the world in general. All that remained for the White Sox then was the hope to square accounts with the Yankees in such meetings as were left for the season.

In the race's next to closing week, there remained championship hopes for Cleveland, New York, and Boston. The White Sox having found their 1951 level, which was fourth place, could hardly wait for the three games they had remaining in the Yankee Stadium.

While they were at Boston, doing nothing to disrupt

the Red Sox plans for getting into the photo finish, the Yankees flattened the Indians in two straight games, and succeeded to the American League leadership by a scant margin.

Coming into Yankee Stadium, the White Sox were in perfect frame, mentally and physically, to play havoc with the Yankees' pennant chances, and thus exact vengeance for the wrong they still felt had been done them on that memorable rainy night during their previous visit. The three-club race for the championship was now so close that every game had utmost significance. Two victories out of three, or a clean sweep of the series would have been all the White Sox desired.

They made a bold start, winning the first game, 7 to 1. Billy Pierce was a superb pitcher and for seven innings went along at a 1 to 1 clip with Vic Raschi, one of the Yankees' best. In the eighth inning, the break came. Two Yankee errors, some robust hitting, notably by Nellie Fox and Ed Stewart, sent six runs clattering across the plate.

Cleveland, winning over the Red Sox, while this was taking place, was again within a few percentage points of the lead, and the White Sox were determined to make it two in a row.

However, these Yankees were not to be thrown into disorder. In Stengel's two previous years, championships had come to them the hard way. This 1951 fight was nothing new. They were geared for it, perhaps better than any of their rivals.

They smashed back in the second game and thanks to home runs by Gil McDougald and Mickey Mantle, the latter's following a wild spell by Lou Kretlow, the White Sox pitcher, victory went to the Yankees, 5 to 3.

Worthy of note was the fact that after Tom Morgan's two ineffective innings, the Yankee pitching was in charge of Bob Kuzava, one of two former White Sox pitchers then gracing the New York scene. The other was Ed Lopat, so long established at the Stadium, many had forgotten he had been traded to the Yankees by the White Sox.

As the Yankees evened this final series, Cleveland again defeated the Red Sox, so the race remained too close for Yankee comfort.

For the third game, Manager Paul Richards had the well rested Saul Rogovin ready. He had not worked in ten days. He had beaten the Yankees three times during the season, and in two other games he had yielded by scant margins only after a mighty struggle.

Manager Casey Stengel of the Yankees had to look beyond the final game with the White Sox, to the three to be played at Fenway Park, in which the Yankees had been unable to win a single game thus far in the season. Stengel gambled on the veteran Johnny Sain, who did not survive the first inning, two runs being scored off him. Rogovin, for all of his rest, was unsteady at the start, and when the Yankees had completed their first inning the score was tied at 2 to 2.

Thus it remained until the fifth inning when Eddie Robinson's triple and Jim Busby's single put the White Sox ahead by one run. They added another in the seventh, when Robinson hit a home run, one more contribution to his seasonal total of twenty-nine, which tied the all-time seasonal high for a White Sox player.

From the second inning through the sixth, Rogovin had not permitted a Yankee to get on base. In the seventh he was reached for a harmless single. It looked then as if the White Sox were within sight of their objective, that of dislodging the Yankees from first place.

The Yankees' eighth began with a hit by Phil Rizzuto. Johnny Mize batted for the pitcher, Bob Hogue, and went out. Here Rogovin had his only control lapse since the first inning and passed Mickey Mantle. Rogovin pitched just twice to Joe Collins. The second pitch was lofted into the right field stands for a three-run homer. The Yankees were on top, 5 to 4. They were still on top at game's end, and, for that matter, at season's end, which seems to be more or less habitual with them.

On the train going to Boston, where Allie Reynolds and Vic Raschi were to gain most important victories, Manager Casey Stengel was being put to the inquisition on what he might expect in the way of Boston pitchers.

"You know," said Casey, "right now I'm not giving that a thought. All I'm doing is being happy I'll not have to look at Pierce or Rogovin any more this year. That kind of pitching makes a manager old before his time."

If the Yankees were not to see either of these two White Sox pitchers again, such was not the fortune of the Cleveland Indians. After they had lost three games in a row to Detroit, a club they had beaten previously sixteen out of seventeen times, the faltering Indians came to Comiskey Park for the season's final game there.

They were defeated once more, Pierce going all the way to accomplish their downfall. This practically wrote off whatever hopes they had left for gaining the American League championship.

In their final 1951 showing at Comiskey Park, then, playing before a final crowd which swelled their home seasonal attendance to 1,328,234 a new all-time high for them, the White Sox more than justified the faith Chicago placed in them. For the first time in thirty-one years the Comiskey dynasty looked into the future with confidence.

As a prelude to the 1952 season, the White Sox provided some excitement in the ordinarily dull baseball month of January. On Sunday night, January 13, an impressive array of baseball-minded folk gathered in the Grand Ball Room of the Palmer House for the 12th Annual Diamond Dinner of the Chicago Chapter of Baseball Writers. Among the guests were Commissioner Ford Frick, American League President Will Harridge, National League President Warren Giles, with representation from many of the major-league clubs. None seemed to be having a gayer time than the White Sox party. Present were Mrs. Grace Comiskey; her daughter, Mrs. Dorothy Comiskey Rigney; her son-in-law, John Rigney; her son, Charles Comiskey II, while important nonmembers of the Comiskey family, but vital factors in the White Sox rise, such as general manager Frank Lane, and manager Paul Richards, were very much in evidence. All were apparently on the very best of terms, one with another.

All the way in from Cuba was Orestes Minoso, there to accept from J. G. Taylor Spink, publisher of the St. Louis *Sporting News,* a gold clock trophy in recognition of having been chosen as Rookie of the Year 1951.

Spink, in a forthright presentation of the history of the *Sporting News* Rookie Award, proceeded to laud Minoso and the White Sox for what they had done in 1951.

Upon accepting the trophy, the unpredictable Minoso launched at once into a rapid-fire speech in Spanish, not pausing for breath for at least a minute, as the startled crowd wondered what this was all about. Without changing expression, Minoso came to a full stop, turned to Spink and said, "Well, anyhow, Mr. Spink, thanks," grinned, and sat down amid one of the evening's greatest ovations.

For this unexpectedly humorous switch on time-honored trophy acceptance speeches, Minoso, individually, and through him the White Sox, helped steal the show with the same rapidity Richards' Raiders had been doing in the 1951 campaign.

It was truly a gala occasion for the White Sox in this, the year of Great Expectations.

The following morning, Chicago newspapers, representatives of which had been commenting upon the happy Comiskey family were notified that Byron M. Getzoff, attorney for Charles A. Comiskey II, had a statement to issue.

The statement, upon being read, precipitated as much of a sensation in American League circles as the one a few years before, when Leslie M. O'Connor's baseball legal joust with the then Commissioner, A. B. Chandler, found the White Sox summarily dismissed from participation in organized baseball.

Attorney Getzoff's statement, to which neither he nor young Comiskey offered to add anything at the moment, read as follows:

> Byron M. Getzoff, attorney for Charles A. Comiskey today announced the resignation of Mr. Comiskey as Vice President and Secretary of the American League Baseball Club of Chicago effective on Friday, January 18, had been tendered to the Board of Directors.
>
> The resignation of Mr. Comiskey represents a long standing dissatisfaction on his part with an inadequate salary and the failure to attain a tenure of office extended to other officials of the ball club not connected with the Comiskey family.
>
> This step was taken as a result of the refusal of the Board of Directors to consider the requests of Mr. Comiskey for a change in his present affiliation with the ball club.
>
> The Board of Directors in response to Mr. Comiskey's resignation has called a meeting on January 18 for the purpose of considering the acceptance of his resignation.

At the moment the Board of Directors had five members, Mrs. Comiskey, Mrs. Rigney, young Comiskey, Thomas J. Sheehan, and Roy Egan. The last two, long-time attorneys for Mrs. Comiskey and the ball club, held no stock in the club. It was popularly believed that Mrs. Comiskey held one-half the shares, with the other half divided equally among young Comiskey, Mrs. Rigney, and Grace L. Comiskey, another sister.

At a supplementary press conference, young Comiskey said that he had no grievance against his mother or his sister, Dorothy, and said that he did not regard his $10,000 annual salary, on what he termed a day-to-day basis, as commensurate with his activity. Though Lane, the general manager, was the only other official of the club not connected with the Comiskey family who had a long-term contract, it was logically accepted that young Comiskey resented this, and perhaps the attention focused on Lane and manager Paul Richards for what they had done to lift the club into recognition as an American League contender. In his press conference young Comiskey stressed the fact that he had nothing but kindliest thoughts for Lane and Richards. His trouble, he said, was with the Board of Directors.

Inasmuch as his mother, his sister Dorothy, and himself constituted three fifths of the Board of Directors, his interviewers had some trouble reconciling this statement with the one that he had no grievance with his mother and his sister.

In between the initial announcement by attorney Getzoff and the January 18 Board meeting, neither Mrs. Comiskey nor Mrs. Rigney had anything to say. Attorney Sheehan was content to remark that in his opinion the young man had been badly advised.

Young Comiskey, as if in resentment of this, then said that unless his attorney, Getzoff, was permitted to sit with him at the Board meeting he would walk out.

Walk out was exactly what he did, within a few minutes after the January 18 meeting was called to order.

246

Very shortly thereafter, the assembled press were read a statement of the findings of the Board of Directors. The resignation of young Comiskey had been accepted. The post of Secretary had been added to the duties of his sister, Mrs. Dorothy Comiskey Rigney. The office of Vice-President was left open.

The formal statement read:

> The Board of Directors of the Chicago White Sox today accepted the resignation of Charles A. Comiskey as vice president and secretary.
>
> Mrs. Dorothy C. Rigney was elected secretary. The office of vice president is to remain vacant.
>
> Mr. Comiskey has complained in the press that his income is inadequate and presented his written resignation. The board reviewed his income for 1951 and finds that his salary and appropriated expense account for the offices he held and his dividends total in excess of $27,000.
>
> The board realizes that Mr. Comiskey has been a decided factor in the success of the White Sox and it is with genuine regret that it is forced to accept his resignation.

So much for the official action which was one more in the long line of events which could happen only to the White Sox.

Mrs. Comiskey, obviously crestfallen at her son's stubbornness sighed, "If he had only sat down and told us what he wanted, everything would have worked out all right."

Young Comiskey, disputing the financial portion of the Board's announcement, said his 1951 income included $4,800 dividends on his 484 shares of stock and that the appropriated expenses totaled $3,500 in addition to his $10,000 salary.

He said that the Board had notified him that if any legal problems arose at the meeting, his attorney, Getzoff, would be recalled, but that he would not be permitted to remain. It was at this point the walkout was staged, while his mother and sister pleaded with him to stay.

Since young Comiskey gave no immediate indication that he would resign as a member of the Board, or sell his stock, the surmise was that the door had been left open for his return, particularly since the office of Vice-President was left vacant.

However, a bewildered Chicago's opinion of the family squabble was best expressed by Tom Duggan, a television sports commentator. He suggested that it was a pity that if the Comiskey family had to have a family row they didn't think of closing the windows so that the neighbors would not be forced to listen to it.

And thus began 1952, the year of Great Expectations. . . .

INDEX

Compiled by Erin M. Riley

250

McInnis, Stuffy, 65
McIntosh, Hugh, 40
McKechnie, Bill, 199
McMahon, Frank, 166, 194
McMullin, Fred, 92, 99, 103, 116
MacDonald, Charles, 107
Mack, Connie, 13, 20, 23, 65, 133, 142, 149, 167, 192
MacPhail, Larry, 202, 203, 220
Magee, Lee, 38, 41, 49, 51, 53, 92
Maharg, Billy, 104, 108, 109, 112
Mahon, John J., 14
Majeski, Hank, 216, 233
major league: joint meetings, 35, 187; off-season play, 61; use of minor clubs, 35; war's halt to play, 76, 77; Zoeterman case, 185–90
Mantle, Mickey, 241, 242
Maranville, Rabbit, 207, 208
Masi, Phil, 216, 234
Mathewson, Christy, 37, 98, 176
Mayer, 92
Merkle, Fred, 38, 49, 51, 52, 53
Merriwell, Dick, 220
Metkovich, George, 216
Meyer, Bill, 233
Michaels, Cass, 207, 218
Milwaukee, 12, 14, 170, 171
Minor, Douglas, 177
minor league, 35; off-season play, 61; pay for players, 127–28; war's halt of play, 61; Zoeterman case, 185–190
Minoso, Orestes "Minny," 163, 222, 224, 226, 227, 228, 229, 230, 231, 233, 234, 244
Miracle(s) of 35th Street, 229, 230, 232
Mitchell, Clarence, 19
Mize, Johnny, 125, 242

Moran, Pat, 89
Morgan, Tom, 241
Moses, Wally, 163
Mostil, Johnny, 85, 147, 200
Mulbry, Walter, 187
Mullen, James C., 136
Mullin, George, 154
Munzel, Edgar, 209
Murphy, 92
Murray, Ray, 227, 228
Musial, Stan, 232

National Commission: abolition of, 113, 115; actions of, 76, 78–81, 104, 113–14, 165, 185; chairmen, 76, 78–79, 104, 113–14; creation of, 77; profit of, 93
National Federation of State High School Associations, 182, 183, 186, 187, 188, 189
National League: actions, 11, 12–13, 15, 204; chairmen, 14; president, 77; profits of, 14, 15, 93; structure, 8, 10, 12, 16
Neale, Greasy, 87, 88, 89, 92, 93, 99
Neil, Paul, 177
New York Giants, 5, 9, 14, 23, 37–53, 70–75, 129–30, 194, 235
New York Yankees, 15–16, 22, 78, 80, 151, 161–62, 203, 208, 235, 237–43. See also Baltimore Orioles
New York gambler, 97, 98, 99
Niarhos, Gus, 234

O'Connor, Leslie M.: general manager, 167–69, 175, 177, 181–90, 195, 196, 197, 200, 201; retirement, 165–66, 195–96; secretary to the Commissioner, 164–65; Zoeterman case, 181–90

Ruether, Walter "Dutch," 87, 88, 90, 91, 92, 93
Russell, Reb, 73
Ruth, Babe, 28, 31, 85–86, 124, 125, 126, 143
Ryan, Jack, 209

Sain, Johnny, 242
Sallee, Slim, 71, 74, 88, 89, 91, 92, 93, 97, 100
Salveson, Jack, 151
San Francisco club, 127
Sanhuber, Charles, 177
Scarborough, Ray, 218, 222, 223
Schafer, Germany, 39, 53
Schalk, Ray: 1919 season, 84, 85; 1921 season, 123; "Black Sox" scandal, 98, 99, 116, 117, 118, 119; fan respect, 137, 155; manager, 134; scout, 130, 178; trade, 34; Walsh-Schalk relationship, 35; World Series, 1919, 89, 90, 91, 92, 92
Schulte, Frank, 24
Schupp, Ferdie, 71, 72
Scott, Evert, 85
Scott, Jim, 39, 46, 48, 51, 53, 62, 68, 70
scouts, 163–64, 177–78, 180, 200, 228
Seeds, Bob, 151
Seery, Pat, 192
Selee, Frank, 17, 18
Selkirk, George, 151
Seneker, George, 177
Sewell, Luke, 149
Seymour, Cy, 15
Shea, Frank, 238
Shea, Mervyn, 178
Sheehan, Jack, 178
Sheehan, Thomas J., 245, 246

Sheely, Earl, 132
Shellenback, Frank, 19
Sheridan, Jack, 39, 41
Shibe, Ben, 13
Shires, Arthur "the Great," 135
Shore, Ernie, 125
Shotton, Burt, 167, 199
Simmons, Al, 33, 142, 143, 149, 150, 163
Sioux City club, 10
Sisler, George, 215
Slight, 52
Smith, 92
Smith, Edgar, 158, 159
Smith, Frank, 20, 21, 29, 30
Soar, Hank, 237, 238, 239
Solters, Moose, 159
Somers, Charles W., 13, 66
Spalding, A.G., 36, 56
Speaker, Tris, 39, 41, 53, 67, 86, 124, 192, 199
Spink, J. G. Taylor, 244
spring exhibition, 61, 128, 193, 224
spring training, 18, 19, 28, 29, 61, 128, 131–32, 164, 224–25
Stamford Bridge, 44, 48, 49, 50, 54
Steinbacher, Henry, 157
Stengel, Casey, 200, 208, 232, 237, 238, 241, 242, 243
Stewart, Ed, 241
St. Louis Browns, 8, 9, 14, 149, 165
St. Paul club, 10, 11
Stratton, Monte, 149, 151, 157
Strub, Charles H., 127
Stricklett, Elmer, 18, 19
Sullivan, Billy, 20, 24, 32, 64, 155, 176
Sullivan, Ted, 7

Tannehill, Lee, 23
Tener, John K., 77